Federal Budget Deficits

Federal Budget Deficits

An Economic Analysis

Richard J. Cebula
Emory University

Lexington Books
D.C. Heath and Company/Lexington, Massachusetts/Toronto

Library of Congress Cataloging-in-Publication Data

Cebula, Richard J.
  Federal budget deficits.

  Includes index.
  1. Budget deficits—United States. I. Title.
HJ2052.C43   1987   339.5'23   86–45792
ISBN 0–669–11095–7 (alk. paper)

Published simultaneously in Canada
Printed in the United States of America
International Standard Book Number: 0–669–11095–7
Library of Congress Catalog Card Number 86–45792

The paper used in this publication meets the minimum requirements of
American National Standard for Information Sciences—Permanence of
Paper for Printed Library Materials, ANSI Z39.48–1984. ∞™

86 87 88 89 90 8 7 6 5 4 3 2 1

To Christie and David and my Mother and Father,
for Their Love

Contents

Figures and Tables

Figures

Tables

Preface and Acknowledgments

The federal budget deficit in the United States has been increasing rapidly since 1981, thus causing growing concern for the adverse economic consequences this deficit could have on the future. Given such concern, it is useful to have a basic understanding of deficits, their possible effects, and their cures. Accordingly, the basic purpose of *Federal Budget Deficits: An Economic Analysis* is to provide the reader with a rudimentary analysis of the potential effects of federal budget deficits; the actual apparent effects of federal budget deficits on the U.S. economy; the potential usefulness of a balanced budget amendment to control the deficit; and the potential usefulness of the Gramm-Rudman-Hollings Act and various other public economic policies to control the deficit.

This book is divided into three parts. Part I is introductory material that attempts to define the objective of the book. Part II is meant strictly for those readers who have had little or no introduction to macroeconomic theory or to the tools of IS and LM. This part consists of four chapters that provide a fundamental analysis of the tools of IS and LM. A basic grasp of these tools is essential to a sound understanding of part III, the core of this book. Readers who are reasonably familiar with the IS-LM paradigms should proceed directly to part III. In part III, we attempt to accomplish the basic objective of the book. In chapter 6, the concept of crowding out is developed at length. The reader is introduced to the basic theories of how deficits allegedly may affect the economy. An empirical analysis of the apparent actual effects of deficits on interest rates in the real world is provided in chapter 7. The possible usefulness of a balanced budget amendment to the United States Constitution is examined in chapter 8. Various forms of such an amendment are considered, along with its drawbacks and limitations. Chapter 9 deals with various other public policies that might potentially be used to control the federal deficit.

This project was undertaken over a two-year period (1985–1986). During this time a number of people have offered useful suggestions. Among these people I especially wish to thank Dick Muth, Bob Conrad, and Milton Kafoglis. I am extremely indebted to Ms. Shayna Blum for data assembly and computer assistance. I also wish to thank David Cebula and Christie Cebula for assistance in data assembly. Finally, I wish to acknowledge Mrs. Nell Sinnock and Mrs. Amy Erbil for their gracious typing efforts.

I
Introductory Statements

1
Introduction

There is a growing concern in the United States for the possible economic problems resulting from rapidly growing and relatively large (by historical standards, in the United States) federal budget deficits. A federal budget deficit is simply a situation in which federal government expenditures are greater than federal government receipts (principally tax collections). When the federal government's income falls short of its spending, the United States Treasury must borrow the difference. It is important to stress that the Treasury does not print money when there is a deficit—it merely borrows the money.

Magnitude of the Deficit

Table 1–1 illustrates the size of the federal government's receipts, outlays, and budget surpluses (+) or deficits (–) for all fiscal years (FY) since 1940.[1] The period of seemingly greatest concern commences, more or less, with the beginning of Reagan's first presidential term. Table 1–1 crudely portrays what seems to be an enormous surge in the deficit size, when measured in current dollars, beginning in FY 1982.

The degree of concern over the federal deficit is exemplified not only by daily news stories (these stories not only reflect concern over the deficit but also are a contributing factor to the concern), but also by various studies that project federal deficits, debt,[2] and interest payments on the national debt. One of the better known studies is the *President's Private Sector Survey on Cost Control* (Grace Commission, 1984). Table 1–2, which provides actual and projected values for deficits, debt, and interest payments for 1980, 1983, 1985, 1990, 1995, and 2000, was generated by this 1984 study. As shown, these projections allege that the deficit in the year 2000 will be thirty-three times the size of the deficit in 1980; the national debt in the year 2000 will be fourteen times the size of the national debt in 1980; and total interest payments on the national debt in the year 2000 will be twenty-nine times the size

Table 1–1
Federal Budget Receipts, Outlays, and Deficits
(in billions of current dollars)

Fiscal Year	Receipts	Outlays	Surplus or Deficit
1940	6.5	9.5	− 2.9
1941	8.7	13.7	− 4.9
1942	14,6	35.1	− 20.5
1943	24.0	78.6	− 54.6
1944	43.7	91.3	− 47.6
1945	45.2	92.7	− 47.6
1946	39.3	55.2	− 15.9
1947	38.5	34.5	4.0
1948	41.6	29.8	11.8
1949	39.4	38.8	.6
1950	39.4	42.6	− 3.1
1951	51.6	45.5	6.1
1952	66.2	67.7	− 1.5
1953	69.6	76.1	− 6.5
1954	69.7	70.9	− 1.2
1955	65.5	68.4	− 3.0
1956	74.6	70.6	3.9
1957	80.0	76.6	3.4
1958	79.6	82.4	− 2.8
1959	79.2	92.1	− 12.8
1960	92.5	92.2	.3
1961	94.4	97.7	− 3.3
1962	99.7	106.8	− 7.1
1963	106.6	111.3	− 4.8
1964	112.6	118.5	− 5.9
1965	116.8	118.2	− 1.4
1966	130.8	134.5	− 3.7
1967	148.8	157.5	− 8.6
1968	153.0	178.1	− 25.2
1969	186.9	183.6	3.2
1970	192.8	195.6	− 2.8
1971	187.1	210.2	− 23.0
1972	207.3	230.7	− 23.4
1973	230.8	245.6	− 14.8
1974	263.2	267.9	− 4.7
1975	279.1	324.2	− 45.2
1976	298.1	364.5	− 66.4
Transition Quarter	81.2	94.2	− 13.0
1977	355.6	400.5	− 44.9
1978	399.7	448.4	− 48.6
1979	463.3	491.0	− 27.7
1980	517.1	576.7	− 59.6
1981	599.3	657.2	− 57.9

1982	617.8	728.4	− 110.6
1983	600.6	796.0	− 195.4
1984	666.5	841.8	− 175.4
1985	736.9	944.6	− 211.9
1986	793.7	972.2	− 178.5

Source: Council of Economic Advisors, 1986, table B–73.

Table 1–2
Federal Debt, Deficit, and Interest on Debt
(in billions of current dollars)

Year	Debt	Deficit	Interest on Debt
1980	914.3	˙59.6	52.5
1983	1,381.9	195.4	87.8
1985	1,823.1	202.8	179.0
1990	3,211.0	386.7	252.3
1995	6,156.7	775.4	540.9
2000	13,020.9	1,966.0	1,520.7

Source: Grace Commission, 1984.

of those same payments in 1980. The accuracy of such projections can of course be questioned. There is no doubt, however, that such forecasts cause great public concern.

There are many ways to analyze the magnitudes of the deficit and the national debt. For example, this analysis can be done in *real* terms, that is, analyzing the deficit and national debt after adjusting them for inflation. This issue is addressed in chapter 9. Nonetheless, two brief remarks seem appropriate. First, inflation reduces the value of the national debt and deficits so that the size of the deficit in current dollars grossly exaggerates the growth of the real national debt. Second, after adjusting deficits for inflation, they are not all as large as they first appeared to be. Table 1–3 portrays the real deficit growth from 1980 to 1985.

An alternative means by which to measure the size of the deficit is to relate it to the level of gross national product (GNP). The GNP level provides an indication of the size of the economy that must finance the deficit. Table 1–4 shows the percentage of the GNP level financing the deficit from 1970 to 1985. Clearly, when measured in this way, the federal budget deficit has grown immensely from an average of 1.818 percent of GNP from 1970 to

Table 1–3
Real Deficit
(in billions of 1982 dollars)

Year	Real Deficit
1980	− 69.55
1981	− 117.68
1982	− 195.4
1983	− 169.09
1984	− 196.01
1985	− 159.76

Table 1–4
GNP Level Financing the Federal Budget Deficit from 1970 to 1985
(in percent)

Year	GNP Level
1970	0.3
1971	2.1
1972	1.9
1973	1.1
1974	0.3
1975	2.8
1976	3.7
1977	2.3
1978	2.2
1979	1.1
1980	2.2
1981	3.6
1982	6.2
1983	5.2
1984	5.6
1985	4.5

1980 to an average of 5.02 percent of GNP from 1981 to 1985. Similar observations can be made with respect to both the national debt and interest payments on the national debt; specifically, the GNP level financing the national debt and the GNP level financing interest payments on the national debt are substantially higher from 1981 to 1985 than from 1970 to 1980.

Objective of the Book

The federal deficit, whether measured in current dollars (as in table 1–1), in real (constant dollar) terms (as in table 1–3), or relative to the GNP level (as in table 1–4), has risen dramatically since 1981. There has indeed been a surge of concern over the possible economic ramifications of the burgeoning federal deficit. Newspaper articles have proclaimed the deficit as the future cause of "death of our Republic."[3] Many proclaim the need for passage of a balanced budget amendment.[4] The Gramm-Rudman-Hollings act was passed in 1985 to provide a format for reducing the deficit to zero by 1991.[5] President Reagan has publicly demanded congressional spending cuts and fiscal responsibility.

To many, federal budget deficits are an economic threat. For example, it is argued by some economists that problems arise when the Treasury borrows to finance a deficit. Specifically, when the Treasury borrows, it floods the bond markets with various forms of government bonds, thus pushing market interest rate yields above what they otherwise would be. Given these higher interest rates, it is then argued by some economists that consumers buy fewer new homes and new automobiles, causing jobs and income to be lost in both the construction and automobile industries. Higher interest rates also discourage firms from investing in new plant and equipment, causing more jobs and income to be lost. In addition, more long-term inflation may result from the reduced rate of capital formation. Furthermore, when interest rates are higher in the United States, the value of the U.S. dollar tends to rise. In turn, this translates into lower exports, higher imports, and thus higher unemployment in the United States. Some economists and financial analysts argue that additional adverse side effects from deficits are also experienced. To some extent, this book (chapters 7 and 9) will address the validity of the arguments summarized above. However, it is important to stress that, while there are many economists who believe in such effects, there are also many economists who dispute these alleged effects of deficits.

Nevertheless, given such concerns about the possible economic effects of the federal deficit, it may be useful to have a basic understanding of deficits, their possible effects, and their cures. Accordingly, the basic purpose of this book is to provide the reader with a rudimentary analysis of the potential effects of federal budget deficits; the actual apparent effects of federal budget deficits on the U.S. economy; the potential usefulness of a balanced budget amendment to control the deficit; and the potential usefulness of the Gramm-Rudman-Hollings Act and various other public economic policies to control the deficit.

This book is divided into three parts. Part I is introductory material that attempts to define the objective of the book. Part II is meant strictly for those readers who have had little or no introduction to macroeconomic theory or to the tools of IS and LM. This part consists of four chapters that provide a fundamental analysis of the tools of IS and LM. A basic grasp of these tools is essential to a sound understanding of part III, the core of this book. Readers who are reasonably familiar with the IS-LM paradigms should proceed directly to part III. In part III, we attempt to accomplish the basic objective of the book. In chapter 6, the concept of crowding out is developed at length.

The reader is introduced to the basic theories of how deficits may affect the economy. An empirical analysis of the apparent actual effects of deficits on interest rates in the real world is provided in chapter 7. The possible usefulness of a balanced budget amendment to the United States Constitution is examined in chapter 8. Various forms of such an amendment are considered, along with its drawbacks and limitations. Chapter 9 deals with various other public policies that might potentially be used to control the federal deficit. These policies include tax policies, spending policies, monetary policies, and legislation (such as the Gramm-Rudman-Hollings Act).

Notes

1. A federal budget surplus is a situation in which federal government receipts exceed federal government outlays.
2. Stated simply, the national debt represents the outstanding borrowings of the federal government.
3. See, for example, Figgie International (1986).
4. This topic is addressed in chapter 8.
5. This topic is addressed in chapter 9.

References

Council of Economic Advisors, 1986. *Economic Report of the President, 1986.* Washington, D.C.: U.S. Government Printing Office.

Figgie International, 1986. Of Debt, Deficits, and the Death of a Republic, *New York Times,* April 20, p. F-9.

Grace Commission, 1984. *President's Private Sector Survey on Cost Control,* Washington, D.C.: U.S. Government Printing Office.

II
Basic Tools

2
The Market for Goods and Services: A Fundamental Analysis

In this chapter, we develop a rudimentary analysis of commodity market equilibrium. *Commodity market equilibrium* refers to the condition of equality between the quantity supplied of goods and services and the quantity demanded of goods and services. This chapter will deal with commodity market equilibrium by developing an analytical tool known as an *IS curve*. Subsequent chapters will introduce more complex behavior and hence deal with more complex forms of IS curves.

Closed versus Open Economies

It is traditional to categorize macroeconomic systems as either closed or open economies. A _closed_ economy consists of economic transactions (demand and supply) that are derived strictly from domestic sources. In other words, a closed economy is characterized by the absence of international trade. A simplified version of such an economy is given by

$$Y = C + I + G \tag{2.1}$$

where Y equals gross national product, C equals aggregate consumer purchases, I equals aggregate gross private domestic investment, and G equals aggregate government expenditures and outlays.

Y is often referred to as gross national product or simply GNP. *GNP* measures the total market value of all newly produced final goods and services produced. For our purposes here, Y is a measure of our society's aggregate production and aggregate income.

Equation 2.1 identifies the key sources of demand for goods and services in the economy as being households, firms, and governments. C consists of all household purchases of new goods and services except new residential structures. The purchase of new residential structures is classified by the United States Department of Commerce as a form of investment. Accordingly, C consists of purchases of services, new nondurable goods (for example, food and clothing), and new durable goods (for example, automobiles or appliances). It is commonplace to refer to C as simply *consumption*. I refers to all purchases by firms of new fixed investment (new plant and equipment) and of net changes in business inventories, as well as household purchases of new residential structures. G refers to outlays by all levels of government (federal, state, and local combined) on newly produced goods and services.

An *open* economy consists of international trade as well as C, I, and G. An open economy is represented here by

$$Y = C + I + G + X - R \qquad (2.2)$$

where X equals exports of goods and services and R equals imports of goods and services.

X represents exports of new goods and services to other nations. As the value of X rises, so does production and hence our aggregate income level, Y. R represents imports of new goods and services from other nations. The more we import, the more we substitute foreign produced goods and services for our own domestically produced goods and services. Hence, imports act to reduce our aggregate production level and thus our aggregate income level. This accounts for the minus sign in front of R in equation 2.2. The net figure (X − R) is referred to as the balance of trade or net exports.

For an open economy, table 2–1 illustrates the relationships between Y, C, I, G, X, and R. Having identified the components of GNP, it is now appropriate to examine some of the basic behavior underlying these same components. The analysis that follows stresses only rudimentary behavior. More sophisticated forms of behavior are dealt with on a selective basis in subsequent chapters.

Consumer Spending

It would be entirely possible to summarize a very rich, intensive, and sophisticated literature on the determinants of consumption, but in order to construct a simple, straightforward, and easily understood model of economic behavior we shall at the outset simply consider a framework where the level of consumption spending depends, given the prices of *all* commodities, principally on the level of disposable income and the interest rate.

Disposable Income

Stated simply, *disposable income* (Yd) refers to the amount of one's gross or *total* income that is left over after paying all taxes. Presumably, the higher one's disposable income, the greater one's purchasing power.

Table 2–1
Components of Gross National Product

Gross National Product (Y)
  Personal Consumption Expenditures (C)
    Durable Goods
    Nondurable Goods
    Services

Gross Private Domestic Investment (I)
  Fixed Investment
    Nonresidential
      Structures
      Producers' Durable Equipment
    Residential
  Change (net) in Business Inventories

Government Purchases of Goods and Services (G)
  Federal
  State plus Local

Net Exports of Goods and Services (X − R)
  Exports (X)
  Imports (R)

The *marginal propensity to consume* (MPC) indicates the amount that consumption spending changes when the level of disposable income changes. This is an important concept from the viewpoint of economic policy formation. For example, assume that a recession exists. As we shall see, one possible form of economic policy might be to cut taxes. The issue immediately arises as to how much taxes should be cut. The objective of a tax cut may be to stimulate consumer spending and thus the economy as a whole. However, if the MPC is small, that is, households are not very responsive to changes in disposable income, the tax cut would have to be quite large to stimulate sufficient spending in order to eliminate the recession. On the other hand, if the MPC is high, the tax cut necessary to end the recession may not be particularly large.

Assuming that consumption depends solely on disposable income, we have

$$C = C(Yd), \qquad (2.3)$$

where Yd equals disposable personal income, that is, income after taxes. Presumably, as Yd rises, so does consumer purchasing power. With more purchasing power, consumers typically increase their comsumption and their saving (S). Accordingly, while C is directly related to Yd, C will typically rise less than Yd in order to accommodate a rising S. As a result, it follows that the marginal propensity to consume lies between zero and unity:

$$0 < \frac{dC}{dYd} < 1. \qquad (2.4)$$

Equation 2.3 is often expressed in linear terms as

$$C = a + bYd, \qquad (2.5)$$

where a equals autonomous consumption and b equals marginal propensity to consume. The term a represents the amount of consumption that occurs even if Yd were equal to zero. Of course, b is the linear form of dC/dYd.

Equations 2.3, 2.4, and 2.5 describe a consumption function. In general, a *consumption function* indicates the relationship between consumption spending and the factors that influence consumption spending. Equations 2.3, 2.4, and 2.5 can be used to describe the type of consumption function emphasized in the classic work of John Maynard Keynes (1936) entitled *The General Theory of Employment, Interest, and Money.* Keynes (1936, chapter 10) stressed the dominant role of disposable income in determining consumption.

Interest Rate

Other factors besides disposable income may exercise a strong influence over consumer spending. Departing from the strict traditional Keynesian interpretation we note that many economists believe, for example, that consumption spending depends not only on disposable income but strongly on the interest rate as well. In this case, the consumption function may take the form

$$C = C(Yd, i), \qquad (2.6)$$

where i equals the interest rate.

The interest rate can be defined in a variety of ways. For present purposes, the interest rate may be viewed as (1) the cost of borrowing and/or (2) a reward for saving. Presumably, then, the higher the interest rate, the greater the cost of borrowing to purchase new automobiles, new appliances, or whatever. As a result, the lower we can expect the level of consumption to be, ceteris paribus. In addition, as the interest rate rises, the reward for saving rises. To the extent that consumers save more (at a given level of disposable income) they spend (consume) less. Accordingly, it can be argued that

$$\frac{\partial C}{\partial i} < 0. \qquad (2.7)$$

The description of equation 2.6 is given in part by equation 2.7 and by

$$0 < \frac{\partial C}{\partial Yd} < 1. \qquad (2.8)$$

$$0 < \frac{\partial C}{\partial Yd} < 1. \tag{2.8}$$

The saving function corresponding to equation 2.6 is described by

$$S = S(Yd, i), \qquad (2.9)$$

where

$$0 < \frac{\partial S}{\partial Yd} < 1, \frac{\partial S}{\partial i} > 0. \qquad (2.10)$$

Equation 2.6 can be written in linear terms as

$$C = a + bYd - di, \qquad (2.11)$$

where $-d$ equals interest sensitivity of consumption. Thus, it follows that $-d$ is the linear form of $\partial C / \partial i$.

Investment

Having developed a basic idea of the meaning of a consumption function, we may now turn to the investment function. An *investment function* indicates the relationship between investment spending (as already defined) and the factors influencing investment spending.

Influence of Aggregate Income

It is commonplace in macroeconomics to assume that investment depends significantly on the level of aggregate income. This may be expressed in the general form

$$I = I(Y). \qquad (2.12)$$

Presumably, as the level of income (GNP) rises in the economy, so does the demand for goods and services. In turn, prices and profits tend to rise. Finally, to adapt to growing demand (market opportunities) and to pursue greater long-term profits, firms tend to step up the pace of investment in new capital. Thus, investment (I) is said to be positively (directly) related to the level of income (Y), ceteris paribus.

The relationship between investment spending and income (GNP) is referred to as the *marginal propensity to invest* (MPI). The MPI indicates the change in investment that results from a change in the level of income and is described by

$$0 < \frac{dI}{dY} < 0. \qquad (2.13)$$

As noted above, the MPI is also less than unity—it would be difficult to imagine investment growing at a rate that absorbs all of GNP. Surely, GNP would rise more rapidly than investment.

Interest Rate

Of course, there are other factors that influence the level of investment. Although the traditional Keynesian argument holds that variations in the interest rate have little or no effect on investment, there are numerous other economists who disagree. Some believe that interest rates exercise a strong, negative impact on investment spending.

To understand the alleged relationship between investment and interest rates, let us consider a firm that is contemplating investment in a new machine. The firm of course is motivated by profits; in other words, the firm is willing to make this investment only if it is profitable to do so.

For each year that the firm operates the machine it can expect to receive certain revenues. These revenues, over the years the machine is in operation, are referred to as a *stream of revenues*. In addition, the firm can expect each year to incur certain costs associated with running the machine, for example, fuel, electricity, worn parts, maintenance, and so forth. All of these costs comprise a *stream of costs*. For a given machine, the difference between the stream of revenues and the stream of costs in a given year is that year's *net returns* from the machine.

Against these net returns that are spread over a period of years, the firm must compare the initial cost (price) of the machine. Obviously, these net returns must include depreciation of the machine. In addition, the stream of net revenues must cover the cost of financing the original purchase. Clearly, if a firm borrows funds from the outside (external financing) in order to purchase the machine, it must pay interest directly; should the firm use its own funds, it must forego alternative opportunities (lose interest on its own funds) and in effect, then, also pay an interest charge for borrowing from itself.

Let us assume that the firm borrows funds from the outside. We then may inquire "at what rate of interest can the firm borrow from the outside, purchase the machine, and still be able to break even?" In more formal terms (to be explained shortly), the question becomes "what interest rate would make the *present value* of the machine's expected future net returns (or *yield*) equal to the initial price of the machine?" This question is pertinent because the firm would be willing to purchase the machine only if the prospective yield exceeds the interest rate at which the firms borrows. The yield on investments is referred to as the *marginal efficiency of capital, efficiency* indicating a rate of net return over cost and *marginal* referring only to *additions* to capital—not to the yield on already existing capital.

If one imagines similar computations for every firm contemplating an investment, one may conceive a marginal efficiency-of-capital schedule for the society as a whole. Thus, let us assume that there are, at a given point in time, $150 billion worth of investment yielding 15 percent or more, $100 billion worth of investment yielding 12 percent, and $100 billion worth of investment yielding 10 percent. Thus, by adding, we can compute the value of the investment projects yielding as much as or more than any given return. Clearly, there are $250 billion worth yielding 12 percent or more, $350 billion worth yielding 10 percent or more, and so forth. This is illustrated in figure 2–1.

One would expect firms to make investments in projects yielding more than the market rate of interest. Therefore, we may turn the marginal efficiency-of-capital schedule around and make it an investment demand schedule. From figure 2–1, we can see that there is $350 billion worth of investment with a marginal efficiency greater than 10 percent. Hence, it

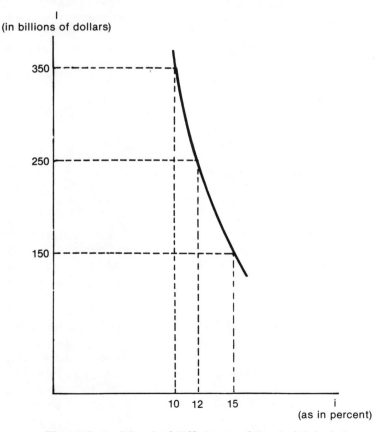

Figure 2–1. Marginal Efficiency-of-Capital Schedule

could be stated that the demand for investment at a market rate of interest of 10 percent is $350 billion. Thus, given the marginal efficiency-of-capital schedule, we can find the value of investment demand if we know the value of the interest rate.

As a consequence, it may be argued that investment is a *function* of the rate of interest, which may be written in the general form

$$I = I(i), \text{ where } \frac{dI}{di} < 0. \tag{2.14}$$

Equation 2.14 indicates that investment depends on and varies inversely with the interest rate.

The basic principles of investment given here do not change if we choose to relax the assumption that all investments are made with borrowed funds. One should not expect firms to invest their own funds in projects that yield less than the market rate of interest since they have other more profitable uses for the money.

Combining equations 2.12 and 2.14 yields the investment function

$$I = I(Y, i), \tag{2.15}$$

where

$$0 < \frac{\partial I}{\partial Y} < 1, \frac{\partial I}{\partial i} < 0. \tag{2.16}$$

Expressed in linear terms equation 2.15 becomes

$$I = I + I_1 - I_2 I, \tag{2.17}$$

where I equals autonomous investment, I_1 equals marginal propensity to invest, and $-I_2$ equals interest sensitivity of investment. Clearly, I_1 is the linear form of $\partial I / \partial Y$, and $-I_2$ is the linear form of $\partial I / \partial i$.

Discounted Present Value

In order to more fully understand the investment decision described above let us reconsider the firm that is contemplating investment in a new machine. Should the firm in fact purchase the machine? The answer to this question hinges on the cost of the new machine relative to the *discounted present value* (DPV) of its future net income.

In order to understand the meaning of the DPV and how to compute it, let us begin by considering the DPV of money. Simply stated, the DPV of money that will not be received until some future time is today's equivalent of that money. For example, if I have $100 today and invest it at 5 percent interest, then one year from now I will have $105. Therefore, today's value, that is, the DPV of $105 *that is not to be received until one year from now* is $100. Similarly, assuming the interest rate once again is 5 percent, the DPV of $1000 that will not be received until one year from today is $952.38. This is another way of stating that if I had $952.38 in my hand today, I could invest it at 5 percent and have $1000 one year from today. The formula that can be used to determine the DPV of a sum of money to be received one year from today is

$$DPV = \frac{M}{1 + i} \qquad (2.18)$$

where M equals the dollar value of the money to be received one year from today and i equals the rate of interest that can be earned.

A variant of the above formula can be used when the money to be received is delayed for more than one year into the future. Suppose I am to receive $100 two years from today. What is the present value of that money today? If I had the money in hand today, then I could invest it and earn interest in two years, and the second year's interest would be *compound* in the sense of being interest earned on interest. For example, $100 invested today at 5 percent becomes $105 one year from now; $105 invested one year from now becomes $105(1 + i) = $105(1.05) = $110.25. The interest earned in the second year ($5.25) is greater than the interest earned in the first year ($5.00) because in the second year I am able to earn interest on the first year's interest. This leads us to a more general formulation for DPV that takes into account the possibility of earning compound interest:

$$DPV = \frac{M}{(1 + i)^t} \qquad (2.19)$$

where t is the number of years in the future that the money will be received.

Using the above formula, we find that the present value of $100 dollars to be received two years from now is

$$DPV = \frac{\$100}{(1 + 0.05)^2} = \frac{\$100}{1.1025} = \$90.70. \qquad (2.20)$$

Thus, we now know that if we had $90.70 in hand today, we could invest it at 5 percent and have $100 two years from today.

DPV and Investment

Now that we are familiarized with the DPV concept, we may return to the case of the firm contemplating investment in a new machine. Let us assume that the machine costs \$10,000, it lasts for exactly one year, and its output can be sold at the end of the year for \$10,000 above out-of-pocket costs. In this case, the marginal efficiency of capital is 10 percent. At this rate, it would be possible to borrow the \$10,000 needed to buy the machine initially, repay the principal (\$10,000) and the interest (\$1000) at the year's end, and break even. Letting π be the expected net return, it then follows that:

$$\text{DPV} = \frac{\pi}{1 + i} \quad \text{or} \quad \$10,000 = \frac{\$11,000}{(1.10)}. \tag{2.21}$$

This investment would be profitable to undertake at any interest rate below 10 percent and unprofitable at any interest rate above 10 percent.

If the machine in question were to yield its \$11,000 only at the end of the second year, then the marginal efficiency would be essentially 4.88 percent. This is because if the money were borrowed at 4.88 percent to buy the machine, there would be \$10,488 (\$10,000 × 1.0488) owing at the end of the first year and \$11,000 (\$10,488 × 1.0488) due at the end of the second year. The formula for such a computation is given by

$$\text{DPV} = \frac{\pi}{(1 + i)^2}. \tag{2.22}$$

If the return had instead come at the end of three years the denominator would have been $(1 + i)^3$; at the end of n years it would have been $(1 + i)^n$.

In reality, of course, most investments do not yield just one return. Rather, they tend to yield returns for each of many years. In such cases, the DPV of the entire stream of net returns is the sum of the present values of each return in the stream. If $\pi_1, \pi_2, \ldots, \pi_n$ are the net returns in years $1, 2, \ldots, n$, respectively, and if $\text{DPV}_1, \text{DPV}_2, \ldots, \text{DPV}_n$ are the respective present values of each of those returns, then the overall DPV is given by

$$\text{DPV} = \text{DPV}_1 + \text{DPV}_2 + \ldots + \text{DPV}_n \tag{2.23}$$

or

$$\text{DPV} = \frac{\pi_1}{(1 + i)} = \frac{\pi_2}{(1 + i)^2} + \ldots + \frac{\pi_n}{(1 + i)^n}. \tag{2.24}$$

The *marginal efficiency of capital* is the value of i that makes the DPV equal to the initial purchase price. To compute i, insert the values of $\pi_1, \pi_2, \ldots, \pi_n$ into equation 2.24, set DPV equal to the purchase price, and then solve for i. At any interest rate below the resulting value for i, the investment would be judged as profitable to undertake.

Observe that the higher the interest rate, the larger the denominators on the right-hand side of equation 2.24. In other words, the higher the interest rate, the lower the DPV. Conversely, the lower the interest rate, the higher the DPV.

Imagine now that we have a relatively high interest rate, such that the DPV is less than the cost of the machine. The firm would refuse to buy the machine since doing so would ultimately reduce its profits. However, if the interest rate were to decline, then the DPV would rise. If the interest rate were to continue falling, then ultimately, we might end up with the DPV being greater than the cost of the machine. If this were to be the case, the firm would definitely wish to purchase the machine (invest). Hence, we conclude that a lower rate of interest tends to induce more investment by the firm. This confirms equation 2.14.

Closing Remarks on Investment

In closing this section of the chapter it should again be stressed that the net returns (the π values) are *expected* future net returns. In reality, such returns are difficult to predict; moreover, the returns are likely to vary greatly with changing business conditions (for example, they may decline with the onset of recession). Furthermore, a firm is faced with several interest rates in different security and bond markets, a fact that can further complicate the computation of the DPV. On the other hand, such interest rates will ordinarily move together, that is, in the same direction when there is a change in the economy's monetary conditions. Hence, we can treat the interest rates as one generalized (average) interest rate value, i. Incidentally, this remark applies to the consumption function as well as to the investment function.

Government Sector

To describe the government sector, we need to consider both taxes and expenditures by governments. As for taxes, there are at least two simple options. First, we may choose to treat taxes as simply exogenous:

$$T = \bar{T}, \tag{2.25}$$

where T equals aggregate tax collections and $\bar{T}$ stands for the exogenous aggregate tax collections level.

Alternatively, we may wish to treat taxes endogenously. For example, let us consider the possibility of an income tax structure:

$$T = T(Y). \tag{2.26}$$

Given positive income tax rate, equation 2.26 is described by

$$0 < \frac{dT}{dY} < 1. \tag{2.27}$$

In equation 2.27 the income tax rate dT/dY is positive but less than 100 percent. Equation 2.27 can be restated in linear form as

$$T = \bar{T} + T_1 Y, \tag{2.28}$$

where T_1 is the linear form of dT/dY and lies between zero and unity:

$$0 < T_1 < 1. \tag{2.29}$$

Government spending can be initially treated as entirely exogenous:

$$G = \bar{G}, \tag{2.30}$$

where $\bar{G}$ represents exogenous aggregate government spending. In this instance, government spending might be viewed as being determined by political factors but not expressly by economic factors.

Should the decision makers in government, say the President and Congress, decide to raise the level of government spending (as defined), then the new level of government spending (G) would be given by

$$G = \bar{G} + \Delta G, \tag{2.31}$$

where

$$\Delta G > 0. \tag{2.32}$$

This change in government spending outlays would be classified as a form of *expansionary* discretionary fiscal policy. If $\Delta G < 0$, the discretionary fiscal policy would be *contractionary*.

Balance of Trade

The balance of trade (net exports) is determined by a wide variety of factors including the domestic GNP, other nations' GNP levels, the exchange rate (value of the U.S. dollar in terms of foreign currencies), the domestic price structure, foreign currencies, foreign prices, and politics. Given the simple objectives of this section of the book, only the effects of income are to be considered here.

Although exports (X) can be reasonably hypothesized as depending on a variety of external (foreign) as well as domestic factors, we shall at the outset simply treat exports as exogenous:

$$X = \bar{X}, \tag{2.33}$$

where $\bar{X}$ represents exogenously determined level of exports. Explicit determinants of exports will be discussed later.

Similarly, whereas imports (R) can be hypothesized as a function of numerous variables, we shall begin by assuming that imports depend on the level of GNP:

$$R = R(Y),$$

where

$$0 < \frac{dR}{dY} < 1. \tag{2.34}$$

It is argued here that as the level of GNP rises, so does the aggregate demand for goods and services. In an open economy some portion of this growing demand is likely to be spent on imported items. The term dR/dY in equation 2.34 is referred to as the *marginal propensity to import*. It indicates the change in imports resulting from a rise in the level of GNP. It is argued to be positive for the aforementioned reason. It is also argued to be less than unity since a nation can hardly spend *all* of its income on imports.

IS Curve

As an aid to understanding the IS curve it is helpful to examine the algebraic solution for the equilibrium level of GNP. Consider, for example, the following closed economic system:

$$Y = C + I + G \tag{2.35}$$

$$C = a + bYd - di \tag{2.36}$$

$$I = \bar{I} + I_1 Y - I_2 i \tag{2.37}$$

$$G = \bar{G} \tag{2.38}$$

$$T = \bar{T} + T_1 Y. \tag{2.39}$$

This very simple system embodies several, although not all, of the relationships discussed earlier in this chapter.

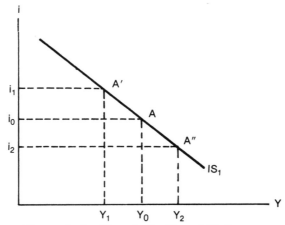

Figure 2–2. Negatively Sloped IS Curve

The equilibrium level of income in this economy is described by the following algebraic solution:

$$Y = \frac{a - b\bar{T} - di + \bar{I} - I_2 i + \bar{G}}{1 - b - I_1 + bT_1}. \tag{2.40}$$

Refer now to figure 2–2, where the interest rate (i) is plotted vertically and the level of income (Y) is plotted along the horizontal axis. Note that both i and Y are in equation 2.40.

Obviously, we can arithmetically compute the equilibrium level of Y in equation 2.40 as long as we have the numerical values of all the economic terms on the right-hand side of the equation. Let us assume that we have all of this information *excluding* the value of the interest rate. The numerical value of Y will then be computable only if we learn the value of the interest rate.

Let us assume that we suddenly learn that the interest rate is the value i_0. Given this, we can substitute the numerical value i_0 into equation 2.40, combine it with all of the other numerical information we have, and arithmetically compute the equilibrium value of Y. Let this equilibrium value of Y be given by Y_0. We may record i_0 and Y_0 in figure 2–2 at point A. Point A, which has the coordinates Y_0, i_0 is then one combination of the level of income and the interest rate that can permit us to have commodity market equilibrium.

Thus, at point A, we have the following condition:

$$Y_0 = \frac{a - b\bar{T} - di_0 + \bar{I} - I_2 i_0 + \bar{G}}{1 - b - I_1 + bT_1}. \tag{2.41}$$

Consider now what would happen if the interest rate were i_1, where $i_1 > i_0$. Substituting i_1 into equation 2.41 in place of i_0, we find that

$$Y_0 > \frac{a - b\bar{T} - di_1 + \bar{I} - I_2 i_1 + \bar{G}}{1 - b - I_1 + bT_1}. \qquad (2.42)$$

Clearly, with the interest rate at value i_1, we no longer have commodity market equilibrium at income level Y_0 since, at Y_0, GNP is no longer equal to our algebraic ratio. In economic terms, what has happened is quite simple. A rise in the interest rate has cut both consumption and investment; hence the level of GNP (Y_0) exceeds the level of aggregate demand for goods and services.

Can commodity market equilibrium be possible then if the interest rate is at the value of i_1? Yes! Clearly, in order to restore commodity market equilibrium it is necessary to eliminate the inequality in equation 2.42. We may now ask the question, given that the two variables plotted in figure 2–2 are Y and i, "what must happen to the level of income (Y) in order to restore commodity market equilibrium?"

Given the inequality in equation 2.42 and given that the interest rate is i_1, in order to restore commodity market equilibrium the level of Y must fall. As Y falls, the size of the inequality in equation 2.42 diminishes and, if Y falls enough, the inequality will disappear. Let the income level at which the inequality disappears be given by value Y_1. We may record Y_1 and i_1 in figure 2–2. Point A', which has the coordinates Y_1, i_1, is thus another combination of the level of income and the interest rate that can permit us to have commodity market equilibrium.

Thus, at point A', we have the following condition:

$$Y_1 = \frac{a - b\bar{T} - di_1 + \bar{I} - I_2 i_1 + \bar{G}}{1 - b - I_1 + bT_1}. \qquad (2.43)$$

Let us now reconsider point A where we have the condition

$$Y_0 = \frac{a - b\bar{T} - di_0 + \bar{I} - I_2 i_0 + \bar{G}}{1 - b - I_1 + bT_1}. \qquad (2.44)$$

Consider now what would happen if the interest rate fell to i_2, where $i_2 < i_0$. Substituting i_2 into equation 2.41 in place of i_0, we find that

$$Y_0 < \frac{a - b\bar{T} - di_2 + \bar{I} - I_2 i_2 + \bar{G}}{1 - b - I_1 + bT_1}. \qquad (2.45)$$

Clearly, with the interest rate at value i_2, we no longer have commodity market equilibrium at income level Y_0 since, at Y_0, GNP is no longer equal to our algebraic ratio. In economic terms, what has happened is really very easily understood. As the interest rate fell, both consumption and investment increased; therefore, the level of GNP (Y_0) is less than the value of aggregate demand for goods and services.

In order to restore commodity market equilibrium at interest rate i_2, we must somehow eliminate the inequality in equation 2.45. We may then ask "what must happen to the level of income (Y) in order to restore commodity market equilibrium?" Given the inequality in equation 2.45 and given the interest rate at value i_2, to restore commodity market equilibrium, Y must rise. As Y rises, the size of the inequality in equation 2.45 diminishes and, if Y rises enough, the inequality will disappear.

Let the income level at which the inequality in equation 2.45 disappears be given by value Y_2. We may record i_2 and Y_2 in figure 2–2. Point A″, which has the coordinates Y_2, i_2, is thus another combination of the level of income and the interest rate that can permit commodity market equilibrium. At point A″, we have the following condition:

$$Y_2 = \frac{a - b\bar{T} - di_2 + \bar{I} - I_2 i_2 + \bar{G}}{1 - b - I_1 + bT_1}. \tag{2.46}$$

If we continue to repeat this process of altering the interest rate and ascertaining what level of income will then permit us to have commodity market equilibrium, we will derive what is known as an IS curve. In general, an *IS curve* represents the various combinations of the level of income (Y) and the rate of interest (i) that can permit commodity market equilibrium. The IS curve represents graphically the behavior of the commodity market. It represents the economic interactions among households, firms, and governments in terms of GNP and the interest rate as the economy converges toward an equilibrium between the aggregate quantities supplied and demanded of goods and services.

Several comments regarding the IS curve are now pertinent. First, the IS curve derived above in figure 2–2 was *negatively* sloped. It should be noted, however, that, depending on the characteristics of the behavioral patterns in an economy, the IS curve can potentially be *horizontal, positively sloped,* or even *vertical*.[1] More is said about this issue at the end of the chapter.

Second, observe that there are many points (technically, an infinite number) along an IS curve. Each one of these points is a combination of i and Y that can permit commodity market equilibrium. However, until we know the actual level of the interest rate, we cannot know (compute) the actual level of GNP in the economy. Incidentally, chapter 3 describes the basics of interest rate determination.

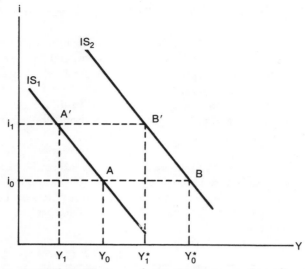

Figure 2–3. Shift in IS Curve from Government Spending Increase

Third, in deriving the IS curve in figure 2–2, note that we did not change either the level of government spending or the tax rate. That is, along an IS curve discretionary fiscal policy is unchanged. It follows, then, that if we change fiscal policy the IS curve may be affected.

Let us give an example of this. Consider figure 2–3, where i is plotted vertically and Y is plotted horizontally. The curve IS_1 is identical to the curve IS_1 derived in figure 2–2. Along IS_1, the income tax rate is T_1 and the level of government spending is $\bar{G}$. Focus now on point A in figure 2–2. At point A, as already noted, we have the condition

$$Y_0 = \frac{a - b\bar{T} - di_0 + \bar{I} - I_2 i_0 + \bar{G}}{1 - b - I_1 + bT_1}. \tag{2.47}$$

Still focusing on point A, let the level of government spending now rise by the amount ΔG, to the total $\bar{G} + \Delta G$. Substituting $\bar{G} + \Delta G$ for $\bar{G}$ in equation 2.47, we find that

$$Y_0 < \frac{a - b\bar{T} - di_0 + \bar{I}_0 - I_2 i_0 + \bar{G} + \Delta G}{1 - b - I_1 + bT_1}. \tag{2.48}$$

Clearly, at point A, since the level of government spending has been increased to $\bar{G} + \Delta G$, the level of GNP is no longer equal to our algebraic ratio; the aggregate demand for goods and services at point A now exceeds the level of GNP. Hence, at point A, we no longer have commodity market equilibrium.

In order to restore commodity market equilibrium, the inequality in equation 2.48 must be eliminated. Following our procedure above, we once again may ask "what would have to happen to the level of income (Y) in order to restore commodity market equilibrium?" Given the inequality in equation 2.48, to restore commodity market equilibrium, Y must rise. As Y rises, the size of the inequality in equation 2.48 diminishes and, if Y rises enough, the inequality will disappear.

Let the income level at which the inequality in equation 2.48 disappears be given by value Y_0^*. Referring to figure 2–3, consider now point B. Point B, which has the coordinates Y_0^*, i_0, is thus one combination of the income level and the interest rate that can permit commodity market equilibrium, given government spending at the level $\bar{G} + \Delta G$. Thus, at point B we have the following condition:

$$Y_0^* = \frac{a - b\bar{T} - di_0 + \bar{I} - I_2 i_0 + \bar{G} + \Delta G}{1 - b - I_1 + bT_1}. \qquad (2.49)$$

Let us now refer back to our original IS curve, IS_1, in figure 2–3. Consider point A', with coordinates Y_1, i_1. Given the level of government spending at G, A' is (as mentioned earlier) one combination of i and Y that can permit commodity market equilibrium. In particular, at point A we have

$$Y_1 = \frac{a - b\bar{T} - di_1 + \bar{I} - I_2 i_1 + \bar{G}}{1 - b - I_1 + bT_1}. \qquad (2.50)$$

Still focusing on point A', let the level of government spending once again rise by the amount ΔG, to the total $\bar{G} + \Delta G$. Substituting $\bar{G} + \Delta G$ for $\bar{G}$ in equation 2.50 we obtain the result

$$Y_1 < \frac{a - b\bar{T} - di_1 + \bar{I} - I_2 i_1 + \bar{G} + \Delta G}{1 - b - I_1 + bT_1}. \qquad (2.51)$$

Thus, at point A', since government spending rose to the amount $\bar{G} + \Delta G$, the level of GNP is no longer equal to our algebraic ratio: the aggregate demand for goods and services at point A' now exceeds GNP. Hence, point A' is no longer a position of commodity market equilibrium.

In order to restore equilibrium, the inequality in equation 2.51 must be eliminated. Following the procedure used above, we may ask "what would have to happen to the level of income (Y) in order to restore commodity market equilibrium?" Given the inequality in equation 2.51, to restore equilibrium, Y must increase. As Y increases, the size of the inequality in equation 2.51 is diminished; if Y rises enough the inequality will disappear.

Let the income level at which the inequality in equation 2.51 disappears be given by value Y_1^*. Consider now point B' in figure 2–3. Point B', which has the coordinates Y_1^*, i_1, is thus one combination of the income level and the interest rate that can permit commodity market equilibrium, given government spending at the level $\bar{G} + \Delta G$. Thus, at point B', we have the following condition:

$$Y_1^* = \frac{a - b\bar{T} - bi_1 + \bar{I} - I_2 i_1 + \bar{G} + \Delta G}{1 - b - I_1 + bT_1}. \qquad (2.52)$$

We may continue to repeat this process, namely, raising the level of government spending from $\bar{G}$ to $\bar{G} + \Delta G$ and moving from points like A to B and A' to B'. In the end, we generate a new IS curve, a new locus of points that can permit commodity market equilibrium—but at the higher government spending level $\bar{G} + \Delta G$. The new IS curve in our example is shown in figure 2–3 by curve IS_2.

In sum then, for each level of government spending there exists a unique IS curve. In the economy we are now dealing with, a rise in government spending has the effect of shifting the economy's IS curve to the right. If the level of government spending instead had been decreased, the IS curve would of course have been shifted to the left. It is left to the reader to verify that a rise in taxes shifts the IS curve in the same direction as a cut in government spending and a cut in taxes shifts the IS curve in the same direction as a rise in government spending. A word of caution is now appropriate. Since taxes and government spending do not affect the economy in the exact same way, the shifts resulting from tax and government spending changes are quantitatively unequal. The reader can confirm this after examining multiplier analysis (not to be considered at this point; see, however, Samuelson, 1948).

Conclusion

It has been observed above that IS curves can come in a variety of slopes. To determine the slope of an IS curve there is a very simple technique. Although the technique illustrated below is for a closed economy, it can be easily applied to an open economy. Consider the following system:

$$Y = C + I + G \qquad (2.53)$$

$$C = C(Yd, i) \qquad (2.54)$$

$$I = I(Y, i) \qquad (2.55)$$

$$G = \bar{G} \qquad (2.56)$$

$$T = \bar{T} \qquad (2.57)$$

Substituting from equations 2.54 through 2.57 into equation 2.53 yields

$$Y = C(Yd, i) + I(Y, i) + \bar{G}. \tag{2.58}$$

Taking the total differential of equation 2.58 and letting subscripts denote partial differentiation,[2] we get

$$dY = C_Y dY + C_i di + I_Y dY + I_i di + d\bar{G}. \tag{2.59}$$

Regrouping and solving for di/dY with $d\bar{G} = d\bar{T} = 0$ yields

$$\frac{di}{dY} = \frac{1 - C_Y - I_Y}{C_i + I_i}. \tag{2.60}$$

Assuming the same behavioral assumptions as given earlier in this chapter, the slope of the IS curve, shown in equation 2.60, has its sign given according to the following:

$$\frac{di}{dY} = \frac{1 - C_Y - I_Y}{C_i + I_i} \gtreqless 0 \quad \text{as} \quad I_Y \gtreqless 1 - C_Y. \tag{2.61}$$

Thus, the slope of the IS curve in this system may be positive, zero, or negative, as the marginal propensity to invest exceeds, equals, or is less than unity less the MPC (which equals the marginal propensity to save, or MPS, that is,

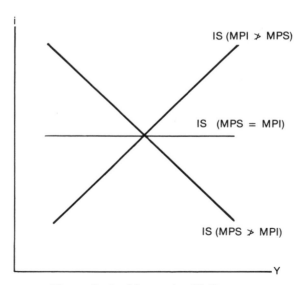

Figure 2–4. Alternative IS Curves

the change in saving resulting from a change in disposable income). These three possible slopes of IS curves are all shown in figure 2–4.[3] Obviously, every economic system has its own economic behavior. Naturally, then, every economic system has its own unique IS curve. Given the behavioral equations for any given system, then, it is necessary to formally derive the IS curve before proceeding to policy analysis.

In closing, it should be noted that C, I, G, X, R, T, and Y are all expressed in real terms.[4] Thus, C, I, G, X, and R all refer to purchases of physical output, and Y refers to real GNP, that is, physical production. Likewise, T represents real tax collections, that is, tax collections expressed in terms of real purchasing power.

Notes

1. Regarding positively sloped IS curves, see Burrows (1974), Cebula (1976), Hicks (1937), and Silber (1971).
2. That is, $I_Y = \partial I / \partial Y$, $C_i = \partial C / \partial i$, and so forth.
3. It should be apparent from equation 2.61 that IS curves need not be linear.
4. Related to this topic, see Smith (1956).

References

Burrows, P., 1974. The Upward Sloping IS Curve and the Control of Income and the Balance of Payments, *Journal of Finance*, June, vol. 29, pp. 955–961.

Cebula, R.J., 1976. A Brief Note on Economic Policy Effectiveness, *Southern Economic Journal*, October, vol 43, pp. 1174–1176.

Hicks, J.R., 1937. Mr. Keynes and the "Classics"; A Suggested Interpretation, *Econometrica*, April, vol. 5, pp. 147–159.

Keynes, J.M., 1936. *The General Theory of Employment, Interest, and Money*. New York: Harcourt, Brace, and Jovanovich.

Patinkin, D. 1948. Price Flexibility and Full Employment, *American Economic Review*, September, vol. 38, pp. 543–564.

Samuelson, P.A., 1948. "The Simple Mathematics of Income Determination, in *Income, Employment and Public Policy*. New York: W.W. Norton and Company, Inc., pp. 133–155.

Silber, W.L., 1971. Monetary Policy Effectiveness: The Case of a Positively Sloped IS Curve, *Journal of Finance*, December, vol. 26, pp. 1077–1982.

Smith, W.L., 1956. A Graphical Exposition of the Complete Keynesian System, *Southern Economic Journal*, October, vol. 23, pp. 115–125.

3
The Market for Money: A Fundamental Analysis

The rate of interest essentially is the *price* paid by the borrower of money to the lender. Whenever the money market is being discussed, the interest rate is also being discussed since anything that influences lending and borrowing generally influences the rate of interest as well. The interest rate already has been considered in chapter 2 because of its possible impact on consumption and investment. Now it is time for us to examine the factors that determine the interest rate.

As noted in chapter 2, consumers and firms are faced with several different interest rates in various security, bond, and loan markets. Since such interest rates ordinarily move in the same general direction in response to a change in the economy's monetary conditions, we can treat them all as one generalized (average) interest rate, i.

Since the interest rate is a form of *price,* its determination will be examined within a supply/demand framework. In particular, after developing and examining the concepts of a *money demand function* and a *money supply,* we shall allow the supply of money to interact with the demand for money to determine the equilibrium level of the interest rate. Subsequently, a new analytical tool known as an LM curve will be developed.

Demand for Money

People want (demand) money for many reasons. Households demand money to purchase goods and services, to hold for future purchases, to meet unforseen contingencies, to avoid the loss that is possible on other forms of wealth (for example, on stocks and bonds), and to have funds available for financial investments when suitable profit opportunities arise. Businesses demand money for some of the same reasons, but are more likely to minimize cash balances in an effort to maximize profits. Governments also demand money, primarily to buy goods and services; however, it is customary in the United States to exclude federal government holdings from the money stock.

Generally, the demand for money is thought to be determined *principally* by the rate of expenditures on real GNP (Y) and by the rate of interest (i). This may be expressed in general equation form as

$$MD = Md(Y, i), \tag{3.1}$$

where Md represents the quantity demanded of money expressed in real terms, that is, in terms of real purchasing power. Equation 3.1 is referred to as a *money demand function;* that is, it indicates the relationship between the quantity demanded of money in real terms and the factors determining the quantity demanded of money in real terms.

Real GNP and Money Demand

The relationship between the real demand for money and real GNP is expected to be *positive:* to purchase a higher level of real GNP requires a greater quantity of money (in real terms) and to purchase a smaller quantity of real GNP requires a smaller amount of money (in real terms), ceteris paribus.

The positive relationship between the demand for money in real terms and real GNP is generally referred to as the *transactions demand for money.* For a given interest rate level, i_0, the functional relationship between Md and Y need not be linear; mathematically, then, the relationship in question is expressed in general form as

$$\frac{\partial Md}{\partial Y} > 0. \tag{3.2}$$

Figure 3–1 depicts one possible form of this positive (direct) relationship between Md and Y.

The transactions demand for money (in real terms) derives from the simple fact that households and firms require money to purchase *physical* output, that is, physical goods and services. Thus, the demand for money is expressed in terms of real purchasing power. If nominal prices of goods and services rise while the physical quantity demanded remains unchanged, the number of dollars (nominal) demanded rises in proportion to prices, but the real quantity demanded of money for transactions purposes is obviously unchanged. The real transactions demand for money changes only in response to a change in real GNP, that is, in response to a change in the level of physical output.[1]

Interest Rates and Money Demand

The relationship between the real demand for money (Md) and the interest rate (i) is generally assumed to be *inverse*. In other words, ceteris paribus, the

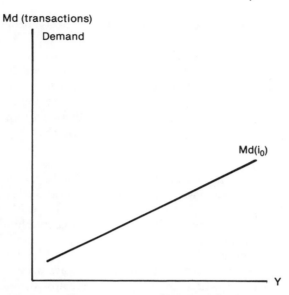

Figure 3–1. Transactions Demand for Money

lower the interest rate becomes, the greater the real quantity of money that is demanded. Conversely, the higher the rate of interest becomes, the less the real quantity of money that is demanded. There are several ways in which to explain this inverse relationship between *Md* and *i*. The explanation that follows is as simply stated as possible.

We begin by observing that people may hold their wealth in many different forms such as savings accounts, certificates of deposit, U.S. Government bonds, corporate issued stocks and bonds, IRAs, and so forth. They may also hold part of their wealth in the form of money.

Money is generally considered to be different from other forms of wealth in three important ways. First, observe that holding one's wealth in forms other than money involves risk—risk of default or loss in value. For example, if one purchases a stock, the value (price) of the stock may decline. This kind of risk does not exist with money, however. In particular, barring inflation, which will lessen the value of money, there is thought to be no risk involved in holding wealth in the form of money. Thus, by holding wealth in the form of money, people can avoid risk associated with other forms of wealth. Thus, we have a risk aversion motive for holding wealth in the form of money.[2]

Second, only money can be spent directly. Other wealth forms must first be converted into money before spending can occur. This means that in order to allow for unforeseen business opportunities people may wish to hold at least some of their wealth in the form of money. In other words, having idle funds (money) around may be viewed as desirable because people will then be able to take advantage of unforeseen business opportunities that might arise but be unattainable unless sufficient money was immediately available. If a good business opportunity was to arise and the individual had either no money or insufficient money quickly available, other forms of wealth might have to be sold in order to get the needed funds. But, selling off other wealth forms might be risky: large losses might occur if forced to sell stocks and bonds on short notice. Having wealth in money form thus helps one to lessen this kind of risk of loss.

Third, when one holds onto assets in the form of money, one either receives no interest or other earnings at all on that money, or usually receives less interest on earnings than is generally and readily available in the financial marketplace. Hence, persons holding any part of their wealth in the form of money may view the interest rate, in a sense, as the cost of holding money in terms of income foregone.

Consider now figure 3–2, where i is plotted vertically and Md is plotted horizontally. Let the interest rate initially be at the value i_0 and the volume of money held as wealth be Md_0. Let the interest rate now increase to i_1. If the interest rate increases, the cost of holding onto money in terms of foregone income rises; continuing to hold onto the same amount of idle money now means that more income is foregone (since the interest rate is higher) than before. Thus, people can be expected to convert some of their money holdings into wealth forms that pay this higher rate of interest. Thus, a higher rate of interest can be expected to result in a smaller real quantity demanded of money, say Md_1.

Raising the interest rate further in this fashion can be expected to result in further declines in the quantity demanded of money in real terms. Presumably, then, we can trace a real money demand curve such as curve $D(Y_0)$ in figure 3–2. Clearly, for the given real GNP level, Y_0, this curve shows the inverse relationship between Md and i. This inverse relationship is sometimes referred to as the *asset demand for money*.[3] Naturally, the relationship between Md and i need not be linear; hence, the general form of this relationship can be expressed as

$$\frac{\partial Md}{\partial i} < 0. \tag{3.3}$$

It is possible to rewrite equations 3.1, 3.2, and 3.3 in linear terms as follows

$$Md = L_0 + L_1 Y - L_2 i, \tag{3.4}$$

where L_0 is the exogenous component of real money demand, $+L_1$ is the

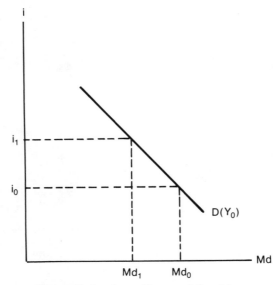

Figure 3–2. Asset Demand for Money

linear form of $\partial Md / \partial Y$, and $-L_2$ is the linear form of $\partial Md / \partial i$. Note that in this equation the positive relationship between Md and Y is captured. A rise in Y results in a rise in Md. In addition, equation 3.4 indicates the inverse relationship between Md and i. A rise in i diminishes the value of Md.

The term $+L_1$ is defined as the income sensitivity of transactions money demand; that is, it is the change in transactions money demand (in real terms) resulting from a change in real GNP. The term $-L_2$ is the interest sensitivity of the asset demand for money; that is, it is the change in asset money demand (in real terms) resulting from an interest rate change.

Tables 3–1 and 3–2 illustrate, using hypothetical data, how the terms $+L_1$ and $-L_2$ are computed. Table 3–1 indicates, for the hypothetical data provided, that $+L_1 = 1/2$. Table 3–1 indicates, for the hypothetical data provided, that $-L_2 = -1000$.

Supply of Money

In most countries there exists an arm of the central government that has the power to control the size of the nominal money supply. In the United States, the agency vested with this power is the Federal Reserve System (FED). This agency can use a number of tools at its disposal to influence the size and growth of the money supply. The principal tools are reserve requirement

Table 3–1
Computing L_1

Y	ΔY	Md (for transactions)	ΔMd	$\dfrac{\Delta Md}{\Delta Y} = L_1$
100		50		
	100		50	$\dfrac{50}{100} = \dfrac{1}{2}$
100		100		
	100		50	$\dfrac{50}{100} = \dfrac{1}{2}$
300		150		
	100		50	$\dfrac{50}{100} = \dfrac{1}{2}$
400		200		

Table 3–2
Computing $-L_2$

i	Δi	Md (as an asset)	ΔMd	$\dfrac{\Delta Md}{\theta Y} = L_2$
.16		0		
	$-.02$		20	$\dfrac{20}{-.02} = -1000$
.14		20		
	$-.02$		20	$\dfrac{20}{-.02} = -1000$
.12		40		
	$-.02$		20	$\dfrac{20}{-.02} = -1000$
.10		60		
	$-.02$		20	$\dfrac{20}{-.02} = -1000$
.8		80		

changes, discount rate changes, and open market operations. *Monetary policy* refers to changes in the money supply or its rate of growth over time resulting principally from the exercise of these three tools. Monetary policy is undertaken by the two main decision-making components of the FED, namely, the Federal Reserve Board of Governors and the Federal Open

Market Committee. The Federal Reserve Board of Governors is responsible for decisions on reserve requirement changes and discount rate changes. The Federal Open Market Committee decides on open market operations.

Nominal Money Supply

The FED uses its monetary policy tools to change the excess reserves of the commercial banking system and thereby control the money supply. We may thus argue that the money supply is determined by the FED. While this is materially a valid observation, it is not entirely accurate; other factors do impact measurably on the money supply. Nevertheless, in the interest of simplicity, it is argued that

$$Ms = \bar{M}, \tag{3.5}$$

where Ms equals the nominal money supply and $\bar{M}$ represents exogenously determined nominal money supply.

The graphical representation of equation (3.5) is shown in figure 3–3, where the interest rate (i) is plotted vertically and the quantity of dollars in the nominal money supply (Ms) is plotted horizontally. As shown, in this simple economy if the interest rate rises or falls there is no resulting change in the nominal money supply. Thus, the money supply (nominal) schedule is perfectly vertical.

If the FED should cut the reserve requirement, cut the discount rate, or purchase additional U.S. government securities on the open market, the excess reserves of the commercial banking system would likely be increased. This excess reserve increase would raise commercial bank lending ability. As additional loans are then transacted, the nominal money supply would grow. This increase in the nominal money supply is shown in figure 3–4 by a rightward shifting of the vertical money supply schedule from $\bar{M}$ to $\bar{M} + \Delta M$, where ΔM denotes the increase in the nominal money supply resulting from the monetary policy just described. Naturally, a reversal of the above policies would reduce excess reserves and the money supply, thereby eliciting a leftward shift of the money supply schedule.[4]

Real Money Supply

Earlier in this chapter we developed a money demand function. That money demand function was specified in *real* terms to reflect the use of money in purchasing *real* (physical) output. Thus far, this chapter has also described the money supply, but only in *nominal* terms. However, *money market equilibrium* is a condition of equality between the quantity demanded of money in real terms and the quantity supplied of money in real terms. Hence, in order

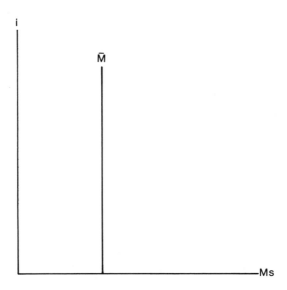

Figure 3–3. Exogenous Nominal Money Supply

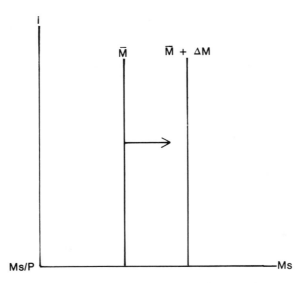

Figure 3–4. Increased Nominal Money Supply

to fully develop the concept of a money market equilibrium, it will now be necessary to make the transition from the nominal money supply to the real money supply.

To describe the real money supply, we simply refer to the following:

$$\frac{Ms}{P} = \frac{\bar{M}}{P},\tag{3.6}$$

where Ms is the nominal money supply, $\bar{M}$ is the exogenously determined nominal money supply, and P is the measure of aggregate price level. In equation 3.6, it is stated that the real money supply, Ms/P, is determined by FED policy ($\bar{M}$) and the level of prices (P). Consider now figure 3–5, where the interest rate is plotted vertically and the real money supply (Ms/P) is plotted horizontally. The schedule M/P in figure 3–5 is vertical to reflect the fact that interest rates do not affect either $\bar{M}$ or $\bar{M}/\bar{P}$. The schedule $(\bar{M} + \Delta M)/\bar{P}$ illustrates, for a given price level ($\bar{P}$), the new (larger) real money supply resulting from a new (larger) nominal money stock brought about by expansionary monetary policy. In addition, note that if Ms were held constant at, say $\bar{M}$, but P were *cut,* then the real money stock schedule would also have shifted to the right to reflect a larger real money supply.

Money Market Equilibrium and the LM Curve

As noted above, money market equilibrium corresponds to an equality of real money demand and real money supply. To address the concept of money market equilibrium, consider the following system:

$$Md = Md(Y, i)\tag{3.7}$$

$$\frac{Ms}{P} = \frac{\bar{M}}{P}\tag{3.8}$$

$$Md = \frac{Ms}{P}.\tag{3.9}$$

Equation 3.7 is the real money demand function and equation 3.8 describes the real money supply. Equation 3.9, which equates real money demand and real money supply, is the condition for money market equilibrium.

Substituting linear forms for the function in equation 3.7 yields

$$Md = L_0 + L_1 Y - L_2 i.\tag{3.10}$$

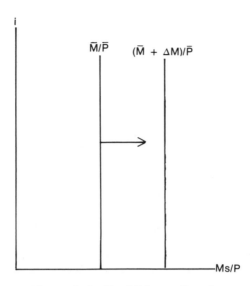

Figure 3–5. Real Money Supply

Substituting equation 3.8 and equation 3.10 into equation 3.9 yields

$$L_0 + L_1 Y - L_2 i = \frac{\bar{M}}{P}. \tag{3.11}$$

Solving equation 3.11 for the interest rate (i) yields

$$i = \frac{L_0 + L_1 Y - \bar{M}/P}{L_2}. \tag{3.12}$$

The interest rate solution in equation 3.12 describes the algebraic value of the equilibrium rate of interest. In other words, the algebraic solution in equation 3.12 describes the interest rate value at which the real demand for money equals the real money supply.

The equilibrium interest rate described in equation 3.12 is graphically shown in figure 3–6, where the quantity of money (in real terms) is plotted horizontally and the interest rate is plotted vertically. Given the real GNP level as Y_0, the aggregate price level as P_0, and the exogenous nominal money stock as $\bar{M}$, the equilibrium interest rate (i_e) is determined as intersection of the real money demand schedule, $Md(Y_0)$, and the real money supply schedule, $\bar{M}/P_0$.

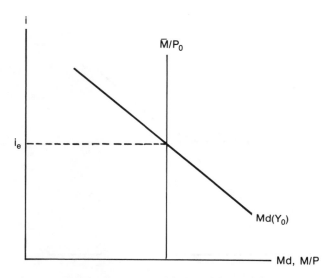

Figure 3–6. Equilibrium Interest Rate

We may now use the analysis impounded in equation 3.12 and in figure 3–6 to derive what is called an LM curve. An *LM curve* indicates, for a given nominal money stock and a given aggregate price level, the various combinations of real GNP (Y) and the interest rate (i) that can yield money market equilibrium.[5]

To begin our analysis, let us assume that

$$P = P_0 \qquad (3.13)$$

$$M = \bar{M} \qquad (3.14)$$

$$Y = Y_0. \qquad (3.15)$$

Substituting from equations 3.13, 3.14, and 3.15 into equation 3.12 yields the equilibrium rate of interest as

$$i_1 = \frac{L_0 + L_1 Y_0 - \bar{M}/P_0}{L_2}. \qquad (3.16)$$

In figure 3–7, let us record the fact that, ceteris paribus,[6] if $Y = Y_0$, then $i = i_0$. In other words, at the coordinates Y_0, i_0 in figure 3–7, the money market is in equilibrium, ceteris paribus.

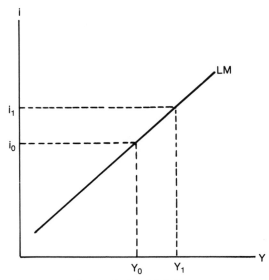

Figure 3–7. LM Curve

Now let Y rise from Y_0 to Y_1. The numerator on the right-hand side of equation 3.16 rises. Accordingly, so does the ratio. As a result, the equilibrium value of i has risen from i_0 to, say, i_1. The point Y_1, i_1 in figure 3–7 now represents a second point at which the money market can be in equilibrium. In economic terms, the higher real GNP level (Y_1) elevates the real demand for money and hence the equilibrium interest rate. In any event, the new equilibrium interest rate is given by

$$i_1 = \frac{L_0 + L_1 Y_1 - \bar{M}/P_0}{L_2}. \qquad (3.17)$$

If alternative real GNP levels are considered, additional new equilibrium interest rates are generated. Eventually the curve LM shown in figure 3–7, is derived. As shown, the LM curve is positively sloped:

$$\frac{di}{dY} = \frac{L_1}{L_2} > 0. \qquad (3.18)$$

Consider now the effects of an exogenous money stock increase, say, from $\bar{M}$ to $\bar{M} + \Delta M$. Given $P = P_0$ and $Y = Y_0$, such an increase implies that

$$i_0 > \frac{L_0 + L_1 Y_0 - (\bar{M} + \Delta M)/P_0}{L_2}. \tag{3.19}$$

Thus, the money market is no longer in equilibrium at interest rate i_0. With the new, larger real money supply, money market equilibrium requires that the interest rate must fall, say to i^*, where

$$i_0 > i^* = \frac{L_0 + L_1 Y_0 - (\bar{M} + \Delta M)/P_0}{L_2}. \tag{3.20}$$

Alternatively, let $P = P_0$ but $Y = Y_1$. If M rises from $\bar{M}$ to $(\bar{M} = \Delta M)$, we have

$$i_1 > \frac{L_0 + L_1 Y_1 - (\bar{M} + \Delta M)/P_0}{L_2}. \tag{3.21}$$

Once again, the excess supply of money forces the interest rate down, in this case from i_1 to i^{**}.

$$i_1 > i^{**} = \frac{L_0 + L_1 Y_1 - (\bar{M} + \Delta M)/P_0}{L_2}. \tag{3.22}$$

The analysis in equations 3.19 through 3.22 indicates that, other things held the same, a rise in M results in a lower equilibrium interest rate. Consider now figure 3–8, where the LM curve from figure 3–7 is replicated. Start at point Y_0, i_0, corresponding to $P = P_0$, $Y = Y_0$, and $M = \bar{M}$. Let M rise to $\bar{M} + \Delta M$. The only way in which money market equilibrium is now possible is if i falls, say to i^*. The new money market equilibrium is then at the coordinates Y_0, i^*. Alternatively, once again holding $P = P_0$, $M = \bar{M}$, but $Y = Y_1$, let the money stock rise $\bar{M} + \Delta M$. Money market equilibrium now requires a new, lower interest rate, say i^{**}. The new money market equilibrium is now at the coordinates Y_1, i^{**}. Connecting points such as Y_0, i^* and Y_1, i^{**} yield the new LM curve, LM'. Hence, other things being the same, an expansionary monetary policy shifts the LM curve downward. Naturally, a monetary policy that contracts the money supply shifts the LM curve upward.

The shift in the LM curve described in the preceding paragraph and in figure 3–8 reflected the impact of a change in the real money stock resulting from a change in the nominal money stock, ceteris paribus. Naturally, if the nominal money stock were held constant, a change in the aggregate price level would also change the real money stock and hence shift the LM curve. For example, a decline in the price level would raise the real money supply

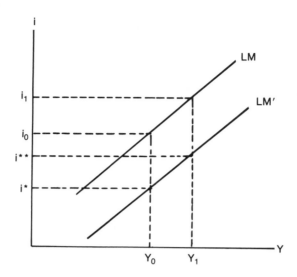

Figure 3–8. Shifting the LM Curve

and shift the LM curve downward, essentially as shown in figure 3–8. Conversely, a rise in the price level would lower the real money stock and shift the LM curve upward.

Concluding Note

Given the system

$$Md = Md(Y, i) \qquad (3.23)$$

$$\frac{Ms}{P} = \frac{\bar{M}}{P} \qquad (3.24)$$

$$Md = \frac{Ms}{P}, \qquad (3.25)$$

the slope of the LM curve, for $dP = dM = 0$, is given by

$$\frac{di}{dY} = -\frac{Md_Y}{Md_i} > 0, \qquad (3.26)$$

where $Md_Y = \partial Md/\partial Y$ and $Md_i = \partial Md/\partial i$. Ordinarily, the LM curve assumes a positive slope.

Notes

1. It should be noted that the demand for money will ordinarily be only a fraction of the rate of expenditures. Since expenditures and income receipts occur over time, the average amount of funds held during a period of time will usually be less than the total amount of expenditures over the time period.

2. Of course, with inflation, one suffers a depreciation in the value of one's holdings of money. Holding onto money, then, involves the risk of losing purchasing power from inflation over time. On the other hand, holding onto various other asset forms does not necessarily guarantee protection from inflation either.

3. Alternatively, it is also referred to as *liquidity preference*.

4. To understand this process in detail, see Klein (1978) and Mayer, Duesenberry, and Aliber (1984).

5. The LM curve was initially developed by Hicks (1937).

6. Ceteris paribus requires that $dP = 0$ and $dM = 0$.

References

Hicks, J., 1937. Mr. Keynes and the "Classics"; A Suggested Interpretation, *Econometrica,* April, vol. 5, pp. 147–159.

Klein, J., 1978. *Money and the Economy,* 4th ed. New York: Harcourt, Brace, and Jovanovich.

Mayer, T., J. Duesenberry, and R. Aliber, 1984. *Money, Banking and the Economy,* 2nd ed. New York: W. W. Norton and Company.

4
Workings of the Fixed-Price Model

I n chapters 2 and 3 the notion of market equilibrium within either a commodity market or a money market was discussed. This chapter addresses the issue of determining both an equilibrium rate of interest and an equilibrium real GNP level for both the commodity and money markets (that is, simultaneously). The first section of the chapter addresses the condition for IS-LM stability. Next, the effects of monetary policy are examined, with both an expansionary policy and a contractionary policy being considered. Finally, the effects of fiscal policy are considered.

To simplify the analysis below, it is assumed that the aggregate price level (P) is fixed. Initially, this will permit us to examine economic policy effectiveness within a more easily understood frame of reference. Moreover, since the determination of the aggregate price level is influenced in part by factors that have not as yet been introduced (see chapter 5), it is appropriate for now to hold the price level constant. Finally, once the tools of aggregate demand and aggregate supply have been formally introduced, the background of this chapter will facilitate the understanding of economic policies within the more complete model.

IS-LM Equilibrium

As indicated in chapter 2, the IS curve corresponding to any economic system indicates the various combinations of the level of real GNP (Y) and the interest rate (i) that can permit commodity market equilibrium. Precisely where along an IS curve the economy is in actual equilibrium is a priori unknown since commodity market equilibrium is expressed simply as one equation (of the form $Y = C + I + G + X - R$) in terms of two unknowns, Y and i.

Similarly, as shown in chapter 3, the LM curve corresponding to any economic system indicates the various combinations of real GNP (Y) and the interest rate (i) that can allow money market equilibrium, that is, equality between the real quantity supplied of money and the real quantity demanded of money. Exactly where along an LM curve the economy is in actual equilibrium is a priori unknown because money market equilibrium is expressed simply as one equation (of the form $Ms/P = Md$), in terms of two unknowns, Y and i.

In an economy consisting of a commodity market and a money market, the entire economy can be in equilibrium only if there is a combination of the level of real GNP (Y) and the interest rate (i) common to both curves. Such a position exists at the intersection of the economy's IS and LM curves.

In order to illustrate a joint (simultaneous) equilibrium in both the commodity and money markets, we consider the following economic system:

$$Y = C + I + G + X - R \tag{4.1}$$

$$C = C(Yd, i) \tag{4.2}$$

$$I = I(Y, i) \tag{4.3}$$

$$G = \bar{G} \tag{4.4}$$

$$T = \bar{T} \tag{4.5}$$

$$X = \bar{X} \tag{4.6}$$

$$R = \bar{R} + R(Y) \tag{4.7}$$

$$Ms/P = Md \tag{4.8}$$

$$Ms = \bar{M} \tag{4.9}$$

$$Md = Md(Y, i). \tag{4.10}$$

Equations 4.1 through 4.7 represent the commodity market. The restrictions placed on the partial derivatives and total derivatives in the commodity market are as follow:

$$1 > \frac{\partial C}{\partial Yd} > 0, \frac{\partial C}{\partial i} < 0 \tag{4.11}$$

$$1 > \frac{\partial I}{\partial Y} > 0, \frac{\partial I}{\partial i} < 0 \tag{4.12}$$

$$1 > \frac{dR}{dY} > 0 \tag{4.13}$$

$$1 > \left(\frac{\partial C}{\partial Yd} + \frac{\partial I}{\partial Y} - \frac{dR}{dy}\right) > 0. \tag{4.14}$$

Restrictions in equations 4.11, 4.12, and 4.13 follow from the analysis in chapter 2, whereas restriction in equation 4.14 is imposed in the interest of simplicity.

Equations 4.8, 4.9, and 4.10 represent the money market. The restrictions imposed on the partial derivatives in equation 4.10 are

$$\frac{\partial Md}{\partial Y} > 0, \frac{\partial Md}{\partial i} < 0. \tag{4.15}$$

Clearly, the signs in equation 4.15 follow directly from the analysis in chapter 3. In addition, our assumption of constant prices (noted above) implies, for the purposes of this chapter, that

$$dP = 0. \tag{4.16}$$

This assumption will be dispensed with beginning in chapter 5.

In his classic article entitled "Liquidity Preference and the Theory of Interest and Money," Professor Franco Modigliani (1944) analyzes the IS-LM framework in great detail. Among other things, Modigliani (1944, p. 63) observes that if an economic system is stable then "each variable approaches some definite value which it will maintain in time until there occurs some change in the form of [a] functional relationship or in some parameter." Working within the context of a simple two-market (commodity and money markets) economy, where the markets are characterized by conventional forms of economic behavior, Modigliani (1944, p. 64) demonstrates that stability of an economic system requires that the slope of the IS curve be algebraically smaller than the slope of the LM curve. This IS-LM stability condition has come to be accepted as valid in the economics literature and is consequently accepted as valid in the analysis here as well.

To illustrate mathematically the source of Modigliani's conclusion as cited above, let us rewrite equations 4.1 through 4.10 as

$$Y = C(Yd, i) + I(Y, i) + \bar{G} + \bar{X} - \bar{R} - R(Y) \tag{4.17}$$

$$\bar{M}/P = Md(Y, i). \tag{4.18}$$

Remembering the assumption that $dP = 0$, we may take the total differentials of equations 4.17 and 4.18. This manipulation yields (where subscripts once again represent partial or total derivatives)

$$dY = C_Y dY + C_i di + I_Y dY + I_i di + d\bar{G} + d\bar{X} - d\bar{R} - R_Y dY \tag{4.19}$$

$$d\bar{M} = Md_Y dY + Md_i di. \tag{4.20}$$

Rewriting equations 4.19 and 4.20 yields

$$-d\bar{G} - d\bar{X} + d\bar{R} = (C_Y + I_Y - R_Y - 1)dY + (C_i + I_i)di \tag{4.21}$$

$$d\bar{M} = Md_Y dY + Md_i di. \tag{4.22}$$

In turn, equations 4.21 and 4.22 can be jointly rewritten in matrix form as

$$\begin{bmatrix} -d\bar{G} - d\bar{X} + d\bar{R} \\ d\bar{M} \end{bmatrix} = \begin{bmatrix} C_Y + I_Y - R_Y - 1 & C_i + I_i \\ Md_Y & Md_i \end{bmatrix} \begin{bmatrix} dY \\ di \end{bmatrix}. \tag{4.23}$$

From equation 4.23, we isolate the following term, which may be referred to as the *coefficient matrix*:

$$\begin{bmatrix} C_Y + I_Y - R_Y - I & C_i + I_i \\ Md_Y & Md_i \end{bmatrix}. \tag{4.24}$$

Stability requires that the real part of the characteristic root of the coefficient matrix be negative. This is known as the *Routh-Hurwitz* stability condition. This condition is fulfilled so long as the determinant of the coefficient matrix in equation 4.24 is positive:

$$\begin{vmatrix} C_Y + I_Y - R_Y - 1 & C_i + I_i \\ Md_Y & Md_i \end{vmatrix} > 0. \tag{4.25}$$

Expanding equation 4.25 yields

$$(C_Y + I_Y - R_Y - 1)(Md_i) - (C_i + I_i)(Md_Y) > 0. \tag{4.26}$$

Rearranging equation 4.26 yields

$$(C_Y + I_Y - R_Y - 1)(Md_i) > (C_i + I_i)(Md_Y). \tag{4.27}$$

Multiplying through by -1 then gives us

$$(1 - C_Y - I_Y + R_Y)(Md_i) < -(C_i + I_i)(Md_Y). \tag{4.28}$$

Dividing both sides of equation 4.28 by Md_i yields

$$\left(1 - C_Y - I_Y + R_Y\right) > -\left(\frac{Md_Y}{Md_i}\right)(C_i + I_i). \tag{4.29}$$

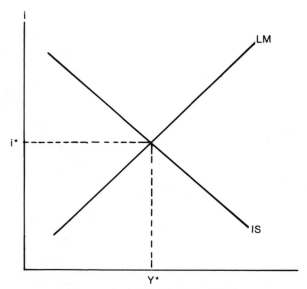

Figure 4–1. IS-LM Equilibrium

Dividing equation 4.29 through by $(C_i + I_i)$ then yields

$$\frac{1 - C_Y - I_Y + R_Y}{C_i + I_i} < \frac{-Md_Y}{Md_i}. \tag{4.30}$$

The reader will recognize the terms in equation 4.30 as the slopes of the IS and LM curves. Thus, as Modigliani (1944) had found, economic stability requires that the LM curve be algebraically steeper than the IS curve. Although Cebula (1976) and others have found exceptions to this condition, we shall view those exceptions as of less relevance for our purposes than Modigliani's findings.

Figure 4–1 illustrates a stable IS-LM equilibrium for the case of a negatively sloped IS curve. At the intersection of curves IS and LM, the equilibrium rate of interest (i^*) and the equilibrium real GNP level (Y^*) are both determined. At this intersection of the curves IS and LM, the money market and commodity market are simultaneously in equilibrium.

Monetary Policy

This section examines the use of monetary policy within the IS-LM context. We shall use the economic system summarized in equations 4.1 through 4.10 for our analysis.

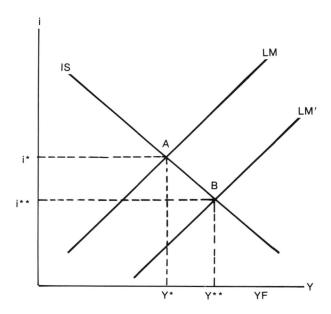

Figure 4–2. Monetary Policy

Refer now to figure 4–2, where the interest rate is plotted vertically and the level of real GNP is plotted horizontally. The economy is assumed to be initially in equilibrium along curves IS and LM at point A, corresponding to real GNP level Y^* and interest rate i^*. Let YF represent the full employment real GNP level, that is, the real GNP level corresponding to full employment in the labor market. (The labor market is explicitly introduced in chapter 5.) Clearly, as shown in figure 4–2, $Y^* < YF$. Accordingly, we shall interpret the equilibrium at point A as corresponding to a recession.

To alleviate the recession, let the monetary authority (the FED) pursue expansionary monetary policies. As noted in chapter 3, the FED has three general tools with which to accomplish this objective: the reserve requirement, the discount rate, and open market operations. Let us assume that, through some combination of reserve requirement cuts, discount rate cuts, and open market purchases, the excess reserves of the commercial banking system are increased. These increased excess reserves raise commercial bank lending ability and hence, to the extent that additional loans are consummated, act to raise the money supply.

In terms of figure 4–2, the expansionary monetary policy described above shifts the LM curve downward to LM'. Such a shift follows logically from the analysis in chapter 3. The increased money supply has the initial effect of reducing the interest rate. As the interest rate falls, the levels of consumer spending and investment spending both increase. With higher levels of consumer spending and investment spending, the real GNP level rises. In turn, a higher GNP level raises disposable income and hence consumer spending; raises investment spending; raises imports, which factor acts to slow the growth in GNP;[1] and raises transactions money demand, which then acts to raise the interest rate and hence to slow even further the expansion in GNP. Note that in this simple economy, monetary policy acts only indirectly on the system, through the interest rate, to raise the GNP level. Note also that, whereas the interest rate initially falls, factors are activated that tend also to raise the interest rate.[2]

In the end a new equilibrium is established at the intersection (point B) of the IS curve with the new LM curve, LM′ . As a result of this policy, figure 4–2 illustrates that the economy ends up at GNP level Y^{**} and interest rate i^{**}. Thus, the expansionary monetary policy has the effect of generating a net increase in GNP and a net decrease in the interest rate. Obviously, the reverse monetary policy, that is, a contractionary monetary policy would have generated the opposite final net effects.

The information provided by the IS-LM paradigm in figure 4–2 enables us to use equations 4.1 through 4.10 to make the forecasts in table 4–1. If the tax structure had included an income tax, such as

$$T = \bar{T} + T(Y), \tag{4.31}$$

where

$$1 > \frac{dT}{dY} > 0, \tag{4.32}$$

then the expansionary monetary policy examined above would have introduced an important additional consideration. In particular, as the GNP level

Table 4–1
Monetary Policy Effects

Forecast	Reason(s)
$C,\uparrow$	$Yd\uparrow$, $i\downarrow$
$I,\uparrow$	$Y\uparrow$, $i\downarrow$
S, unknown without more empirical information	while ($Y\uparrow$) raises, S, ($i\downarrow$) reduces S
G, T, both unchanged	no fiscal policy change
X, unchanged	exports are exogenous
$R,\uparrow$	$Y\uparrow$
$Ms,\uparrow$	monetary policy
$Md,\uparrow$	$Y\uparrow$, $i\downarrow$

was rising, tax collections would be rising, which in turn would act to reduce the growth of disposable income and of consumption.[3] On the one hand, the growing tax collections (by themselves) would tend to generate a budget surplus (or a diminished budget deficit). On the other hand, the existence of the income tax tends to moderate the pattern of GNP growth over time.[4] Indeed, due to this latter characteristic, an income tax is sometimes referred to as a *built-in stabilizer,* that is, a factor in the economy that automatically restrains GNP from rising or falling dramatically.

Fiscal Policy

This section of the chapter examines the use of fiscal policy within the IS-LM framework. Once again, we shall use the economic system summarized in equations 4.1 through 4.10 for our analysis. Reference will be made to changing government spending and to changing taxes.

We begin by referring to figure 4–3, where curves IS and LM intersect at GNP level Y^* and interest rate i^*, that is, at point A. Since $Y^* < YF$, the initial equilibrium once again corresponds to a recession. To alleviate this recession, we shall now use fiscal policy. *Fiscal policy,* for present purposes,

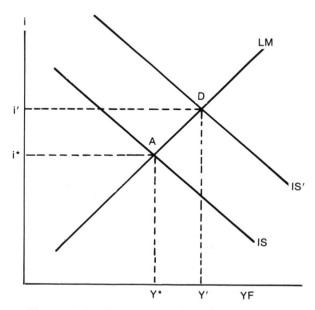

Figure 4–3. Government Spending Increased

refers to changes in the level of government spending or the tax structure. To begin our analysis, let us initially increase the level of government spending in order to combat the recession.

Of course, before the actual level of government spending can rise, the Treasury must obtain the funds to finance the policy. A rise in government spending would tend to generate a deficit unless a large enough surplus already existed. If the Treasury should incur a deficit it would be forced to borrow by issuing U.S. government bonds. Since the effects of deficits and Treasury financing are to be considered later, we shall for the moment simply concentrate on the actual execution of the policy, that is, the actual expenditure increase itself.

As the level of G rises, the IS curve shifts upward to IS$'$. As government spending is increased the level of GNP rises directly.[5] In turn, as the GNP level rises so does investment. In addition, as the GNP level rises the level of disposable income is increased and hence so is the level of consumer spending. The rising GNP also raises imports, which factor acts to slow the subsequent expansion of the GNP level. This process continues on, but as the GNP level is rising the transactions demand for money is increasing as well. This rising money demand in turn elevates interest rates and hence further slows the expansion of consumption and investment and thus the growth of GNP.

Ultimately, the economy ends up at point D, which is the intersection of the LM curve and the new curve IS$'$. The new equilibrium GNP level is Y', and the new equilibrium interest rate is i'. Clearly, the expansionary government spending policy has acted to generate a net rise in the GNP level and a net rise in the interest rate as well. Obviously, the reverse policy, a decline in government spending, would have generated the opposite final net effects.

The results shown in figure 4–3, together with equations 4.1 through 4.10, enable us to make the forecasts in table 4–2.

Table 4–2
Fiscal Policy Effects

Forecast	Reason(s)
C, unknown	as $Yd\uparrow$, $C\uparrow$, but as $i\uparrow$, $C\downarrow$
S,↑	$Yd\uparrow$, $i\uparrow$
I, unknown	as $Y\uparrow$, $I\uparrow$, but as $i\uparrow$, $I\downarrow$
G,↑	policy decision
T, unchanged	no tax policy
X, unchanged	exports are exogenous
R,↑	$Y\uparrow$
Ms, unchanged	no monetary policy change
Md, unchanged	Ms/P is unchanged

Naturally, if equation 4.31 were to replace equation 4.5, then the rising GNP level would raise tax collections. This in turn would reduce the growth of disposable income and consumption, and hence of GNP; and tend at least somewhat to help offset the deficit-creating impact of the increased government spending.

A tax policy would, in this system, have generated many of the same effects as the government spending policy. However, a tax policy works differently from a government spending policy. Whereas a government spending policy may influence GNP directly, a tax policy generally influences GNP indirectly. Specifically, if taxes were decreased the result would be merely an increased disposable income. Only later, sometime after consumer spending rose, would the GNP level rise. Thus, tax policy would change GNP only indirectly through (after) its effects on Yd and C.

Concluding Remarks

Mathematically, the effects on GNP of the policies described above, for the case of a negatively sloped IS curve, are as follows:

$$\frac{dy}{d\bar{M}} = \frac{C_i + I_i}{(1 - C_Y - I_Y + R_Y)Md_i + (C_i + I_i)Md_Y} > 0 \quad (4.33)$$

$$\frac{dy}{d\bar{G}} = \frac{Md_i}{(1 - C_Y - I_Y + R_Y)Md_i + (C_i + I_i)Md_Y} > 0 \quad (4.34)$$

In addition, these results hold for the case of a positively sloped IS curve, that is, one where

$$\frac{(1 - C_Y - I_Y + R_Y)}{C_i + I_i} > 0 \quad (4.35)$$

and

$$(C_i + I_i) < 0. \quad (4.36)$$

Next, the effects on the interest rate of the policies described above, for the case of the negatively sloped IS curve, are given by

$$\frac{di}{d\bar{M}} = \frac{(1 - C_Y - I_Y + R_Y)}{(1 - C_Y - I_Y + R_Y)Md_i + (C_i + I_i)Md_Y} < 0 \quad (4.37)$$

$$\frac{di}{d\bar{G}} = \frac{-Md_Y}{(1 - C_Y - I_Y + R_Y)Md_i + (C_i + I_i)Md_Y} > 0 \quad (4.38)$$

The sign for $di/d\bar{M}$ reverses to positive in the case of the *positively* sloped IS curve.[6] On the other hand, the sign on $di/d\bar{G}$ remains positive for the *positively* sloped IS curve case.[7]

This chapter has provided the fundamentals of economic policy analysis, given $dP = 0$. In the following chapter the price level is allowed to change. This will have important ramifications for i, Y, and the other economic variables in the system.

Notes

1. Recall that a higher level of imports acts to reduce GNP since more foreign production is being substituted for domestic production.
2. Related to this pattern of interest rate changes, see also Patinkin (1965).
3. The fact that the positive income tax rate is less than 100 percent implies that, although taxes are increasing when GNP grows, the disposable income level will nevertheless experience a positive net expansion.
4. This phenomenon whereby the income tax inhibits the growth in GNP is referred to as *fiscal drag*.
5. We are assuming that the government expenditure increase is for newly produced goods and services.
6. With a positively sloped IS curve, $1 - C_Y - I_Y + R_Y < 0$ for $C_Y + I_i < 0$.
7. Related to positively sloped IS curves, see Cebula (1985), Burrows (1974), Silber (1971), Steindl (1970), and Tavlas (1980).

References

Burrows, P., 1974. The Upward Sloping IS Curve and the Control of Income and the Balance of Payments, *Journal of Finance,* June, vol. 29, pp. 955–961.

Cebula, R.J., 1976. A Brief Note on Economic Policy Effectiveness, *Southern Economic Journal,* October, vol. 43, pp. 1174–1176.

Cebula, R.J., 1985. Policy Multipliers and the Slopes of IS and LM: Comment, *Southern Economic Journal,* January, vol. 51, pp. 906–908.

Modigliani, F., 1944. Liquidity Preference and the Theory of Interest and Money, *Econometrica,* January, vol. 12, pp. 45–88.

Patinkin, D., 1965. *Money, Interest, and Prices,* 2nd ed. New York: Harper and Row.

Silber, W.L., 1971. Monetary Policy Effectiveness: The Case of a Positively Sloped IS Curve, *Journal of Finance,* December, vol. 26, pp. 1077–1082.

Steindl, F., 1970. Giffen Goods, IS Curves and Macroeconomic Stability, *Metroeconomica,* May–August, vol. 22, pp. 165–169.

Tavlas, G., 1980. Economic Policy Effectiveness in Hicksian Analysis: An Extension, *Kredit und Kapital,* January, vol. 13, pp. 252–262.

5
The Variable Price Model

T he first section of this chapter develops the aggregate supply curve. An *aggregate supply curve* indicates the quantities supplied to the marketplace of real GNP at various alternative levels of the aggregate price level. Two different versions of the aggregate supply curve are to be developed. The second section of this chapter utilizes the materials in chapters 2 and 3 to derive an aggregate demand curve. An *aggregate demand curve* indicates the quantities of real GNP demanded at various alternative levels of the aggregate price level. Finally, the third section of this chapter briefly examines monetary and fiscal policies with the expanded macroeconomic system.

Aggregate Supply

Thus far, the basic emphasis has been on aggregate demand and on the sources of aggregate demand. It is now time for us to analyze the nature of the aggregate supply of goods and services. To do this, we briefly examine an economy's aggregate production function. Then we analyze the demand for and supply of labor. Finally, we examine the nature of the aggregate supply curve of goods and services under two alternative labor-market structures: a crude Classical labor market and a Keynesian-type labor market.

Labor Market

Despite the heterogeneity of the labor force and of labor services, it is convenient for us to consider labor services as a single, homogeneous input with a single factor price. We assume, for simplicity, that the firms in the economy are perfectly competitive and seek to maximize profits. Consider, then, the behavior of a single such firm. It is confronted with a production function that specifies the given technological relationship between its inputs of productive factors and the resulting outputs of commodities. It is assumed that in the short run the capital equipment of the firm is fixed in amount, so that the firm's sole input utilization problem is to choose its optimum input of labor services. For any real wage rate this input will be that which yields a marginal product equal to the given rate. Thus, the firm's demand curve for labor is the marginal product curve derived from its production function.

If we transfer these concepts to an economy as a whole, we can conceive of a short run aggregate production function. The *short run aggregate production function* for an economy relates the level of real GNP produced to the total input of labor services in the economy (N) and the total (fixed) amount of capital in the economy (K).

An equation for the aggregate short-run production function is given by

$$Y = Y(N, \bar{K}), \qquad (5.1)$$

where $Y'(N, \bar{K}) > 0$ and $Y''(N, \bar{K}) < 0$.

Such a production function is illustrated in figure 5–1. Note that, while it is positively sloped throughout, its slope is nevertheless declining as we move from left to right. This implies the presence of the *Law of Diminishing Returns*.

Let W represent the money wage rate and let P once again be the aggregate price level. Then, at any level of the real wage, W/P, the total volume demanded of labor in the economy must satisfy the following relationship:

$$\frac{W}{P} = Y'(N, \bar{K}), \qquad (5.2)$$

where $Y'(N, \bar{K})$ is the value of the marginal product of labor, given capital stock $\bar{K}$.

The economy's total demand curve for labor can be obtained by inverting the function in equation 5.2 and writing the result as

$$ND = ND(W/P, \bar{K}) \qquad (5.3)$$

where ND is the aggregate amount demanded of labor in the economy. Clearly, if the Law of Diminishing Returns holds (as shown in figure 5–1), then the demand curve for labor is negatively sloped with respect to increases in the real wage rate.

Consider next the supply curve of labor. To the extent that an individual operates on the principle of utility maximization, the amount of labor supplied will depend on the real wage rate. Therefore, we assume that the aggregate supply curve for labor also depends on this rate. Thus, we may write

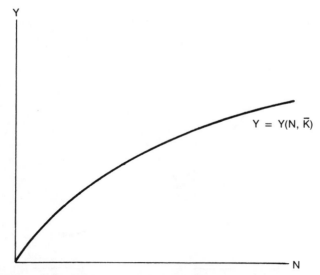

Figure 5–1. Short-Run Aggregate Production Function

$$NS = NS(W/P), \qquad (5.4)$$

where NS is the aggregate amount of labor supplied in the economy. It is assumed here that the supply of labor is strictly an increasing function of the real wage

$$NS'(W/P) > 0. \qquad (5.5)$$

The condition that must be satisfied for the labor market to be in equilibrium is given given by

$$NS = ND \qquad (5.6)$$

That is, the real wage will be an equilibrium one so long as it equates the amounts of labor supplied and demanded. This market is illustrated in figure 5–2. The labor suply curve (NS) intersects the labor demand curve (ND) at point A, which corresponds to an equilibrium real wage of $(W/P)_0$ and to a volume of labor employed of NF. At this real wage level, the quantity supplied of labor precisely equals the quantity demanded of labor. Everyone who is willing and able to work at real wage $(W/P)_0$ is employed; moreover, at $(W/P)_0$, $NS = ND$. Hence, NF represents full employment equilibrium in the labor market.

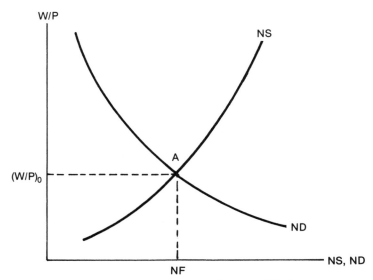

Figure 5–2. Labor Market Equilibrium

It is now timely to make two simple but pertinent observations. First, the real wage rate is merely a ratio of the money wage rate (W) to the price level (P). Hence, there theoretically exist an unlimited number of possible money wage-price level combinations that can produce the same real wage rate. For example, let the real wage rate be (W/P)$_0$, as in figure 5–3; furthermore, let the value of the ratio (W/P)$_0$ be ten units. The real wage rate (W/P)$_0$ then can be described by any of a number of money wage-price combinations:

$$\left(\frac{W}{P}\right)_0 = 10 = \frac{10}{1} = \frac{20}{2} = \frac{30}{3} = \ldots \tag{5.7}$$

Second, if the money wage rate has any given value, say $\bar{W}$, and if the aggregate price level (P) is plotted along one axis of a two-dimensional diagram while the real wage (W/P) is plotted along the other axis of the diagram, the money wage rate is represented by a rectangular hyperbola. Consider figure 5–3. At point A, the aggregate price level is P_1 and the real wage, given the money wage at level $\bar{W}$, is given by ($\bar{W}/P_1$). The product of the price level times the real wage is given by

$$P_1(\bar{W}/P_1) = \bar{W}. \tag{5.8}$$

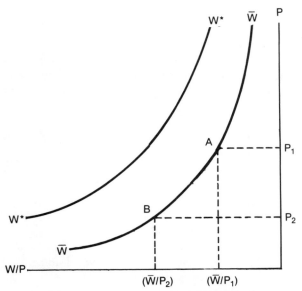

Figure 5–3. Money Wage Hyperbolas

Consider now point B in figure 5–3. The price level is now P_2, and, with the money wage rate still at value $\bar{W}$, the real wage is now ($\bar{W}/P_2$). The product of the price level times the real wage at point B is given by:

$$P_2(\bar{W}/P_2) = \bar{W}. \tag{5.9}$$

All other points along curve $\bar{W}\bar{W}$ have the same trait as points A and B, namely, the product of the price level times the real wage is a constant (in this case, $\bar{W}$). Thus, by definition, the curve $\bar{W}\bar{W}$ in figure 5–3 is a rectangular hyperbola. By the same reasoning, given a higher money wage rate, perhaps W^*, a new rectangular money wage hyperbola could be traced out (see curve W^*W^* in figure 5–3).

We are now in a position to formally derive the aggregate supply curve of goods and services (that is, of real GNP) for an entire economy. We shall do so for two types of labor markets: (1) a Classical labor market in which both money wages and prices are completely flexible, both upward and downward, and (2) a Keynesian-type labor market in which the money wage rate is rigid in the downward direction (for institutional reasons, to be briefly elaborated on later), but flexible upward at full employment, and in which the aggregate price level is entirely flexible (both upward and downward).

Aggregate Supply in a Classical System

Traditionally, the school of economic thought referred to as Classical economics has held that both money wages and prices are entirely flexible, both upward and downward. To obtain some insight into the implications of such flexibilities, we formally use the following to represent the crude Classical labor market:

$$Y = Y(N, \bar{K}), \ Y'(N, \bar{K}) > 0, \ Y''(N, \bar{K}) < 0 \qquad (5.10)$$

$$ND = ND(W/P, \bar{K}), \ ND'(W/P) < 0 \qquad (5.11)$$

$$NS = NS(W/P), \ NS'(W/P) > 0 \qquad (5.12)$$

$$NS(W/P) = ND(W/P, \bar{K}) \qquad (5.13)$$

$$W, P = \text{completely flexible, upward and} \atop \text{downward} \qquad (5.14)$$

Refer now to the four-quadrant diagram (figure 5–4), where these equations are plotted and where we shall presently derive the aggregate supply curve of goods and services (real GNP) corresponding to the Classical labor market.

In quadrant IV of figure 5–4, the production function from equation 5.10 is plotted. In quadrant III, the labor demand and supply curves from equations 5.11 and 5.12 are plotted. Observe that at the intersection of curves NS and ND the employment level is given as NF (full employment), and the equilibrium real wage rate is the ratio $(W/P)_0$. Next, refer to quadrant II, where the real wage is plotted horizontally and the aggregate price level is plotted vertically. Let us assume that the economy is initially at full employment; hence, the real wage rate is the ratio $(W/P)_0$. If the price level was initially given by the value $\bar{P}$, we may ask, "What would the money wage rate have to be in order to yield the full employment real wage rate $(W/P)_0$?" Clearly, if the price level is $\bar{P}$ and the real wage is thus $(W/P)_0 = (W/P)_0$, the only money wage rate compatible with full employment equilibrium is that along the rectangular wage hyperbola that runs through point A in quadrant II, namely, money wage $\bar{W}$. That is, as plotted in quadrant II, we see that

$$\left(\frac{W}{P}\right)_0 = \frac{\bar{W}}{P} \qquad (5.15)$$

for $P = \bar{P}$.

For $P = \bar{P}$, the rectangular hyperbola for any other money wage rate would not run through point A and hence could not be associated with real wage rate $(W/P)_0$.

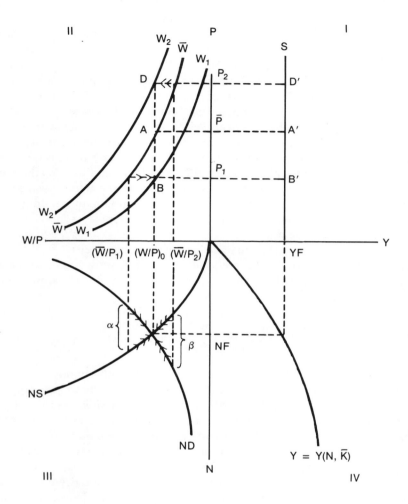

Figure 5–4. Classical Supply Curve

Going further, if full employment prevails and if the price level is given by value $\bar{P}$, then the money wage rate is $\bar{W}$, the real wage is $\bar{W}/\bar{P}$, and the employment level is given by NF. Referring now to quadrant IV, if the employment level is NF, the production function indicates that the level of real GNP produced is value YF. YF is the full employment level of output since it is the value of real output that is produced when the labor force is fully employed. Point A' in quadrant I, with coordinates YF, P, thus indicates that the value of real GNP supplied (produced) at a price level of $\bar{P}$ would be YF.

Consider next the impact of, say, a price decrease, from $\bar{P}$ to P_1. As the price level falls to P_1, the real wage rate rises from $\bar{W}/\bar{P}$ to W/P_1. As the real wage rises, the quantity demanded of labor falls, and the quantity supplied of labor rises. Hence, at real wage (W/P_1), $NS > ND$. This excess supply of labor is shown in quadrant III by distance α. Now, since money wages are entirely flexible in this Classical system, the excess supply of labor then creates effective downward pressure on and movement of the money wage rate. As the money wage rate falls, at price level P_1, the real wage rate also falls. The declining real wage rate is then accompanied by a decline in the quantity of labor supplied and a rise in the quantity of labor demanded. This is shown in quadrant III by arrows along curves NS and ND. In addition, as the money wage rate is falling the economy is moving to lower rectangular wage hyperbolas in quadrant II. The money wage rate will continue to fall until the excess supply of labor has disappeared. The excess supply of labor will have disappeared once the full employment real wage rate ($W/P)_0$ has been restored. This occurs, given the price level at P_1, at a money wage of W_1. The rectangular wage hyperbola corresponding to W_1 is shown in quadrant II as running through point B, with coordinates ($W/P)_0$, P_1. Thus, in terms of quadrant II

$$\left(\frac{W}{P}\right)_0 = \left(\frac{W_1}{P_1}\right) = \left(\frac{\bar{W}}{\bar{P}}\right). \qquad (5.16)$$

Proceeding further, given price level P_1, the full employment money wage rate is W_1 and the employment level is NF. Referring to quadrant IV, if the employment level is NF, the production function indicates that the level of real GNP produced is value YF. Point B′ in quadrant I, then, indicates that the value of real GNP supplied at a price level of P_1 would be YF.

Starting back at point A, consider alternatively the effect of a price increase, say, from $\bar{P}$ to P_2. As the price level rises to P_2, the real wage rate falls from ($\bar{W}/\bar{P}$) to ($\bar{W}/P_2$). As the real wage falls, the quantity demanded of labor rises, and the quantity supplied of labor declines. Hence, at real wage ($\bar{W}/P_2$), $ND > NS$. This excess demand for labor is shown in quadrant III by distance β. Now, since money wages are perfectly flexible in this system, the excess demand for labor creates an effective upward pressure on and movement of the money wage rate (as employers bid against one another to purchase labor services). As the money wage rate rises, at price level P_2 the real wage rises, thereby depressing the quantity demanded of labor and increasing the quantity supplied of labor. This is shown in quadrant III by arrows along curves NS and ND. In addition, as the money wage rate is rising the economy is moving to higher rectangular wage hyperbolas in quadrant II. The money wage rate continues to rise until the excess demand for labor has disappeared. The excess labor demand will have disappeared entirely once the full employment real wage ($W/P)_0$ has been restored. This occurs, given price level P_2, at a money wage of W_2. The rectangular wage hyperbola corresponding to W_2 is shown in quadrant II as running through point D, with coordinates $(W/P)_0$, P_2. Thus, in terms of quadrant II

$$\left(\frac{W}{P}\right)_0 = \left(\frac{W_2}{P_2}\right) = \left(\frac{W_1}{P_1}\right) = \left(\frac{\bar{W}}{\bar{P}}\right). \tag{5.17}$$

Going further, given the price level at P_2, the full employment money wage rate is W_2 and the employment level is NF. If the employment level is NF, the level of real GNP produced is YF. Point D′ in quadrant I, with coordinates YF, P_2, thus indicates that the value of real GNP supplied at a price level of P_2 would be YF.

If we were to repeat this procedure for other prices we would generate additional points such as A′, B′, and D′. As should be quite clear, in this Classical labor market (where money wages and the price level are completely flexible), all such points would lie along a vertical line such as S in quadrant I of figure 5–4. In other words, the aggregate supply curve in the Classical system is perfectly vertical, indicating that regardless of the price level the system will always be able, in equilibrium, to supply the full employment output level, that is, the full employment level of real GNP.

Aggregate Supply in a Keynesian-Type Labor Market

We have just seen that under conditions of perfectly flexible money wages and prices the aggregate supply curve is perfectly vertical. We encounter a very different shape of aggregate supply curve in a Keynesian-type labor market. To formally derive the aggregate supply curve for a Keynesian-type system, we begin with the following familiar equations:

$$Y = Y(N, \bar{K}), \; Y'(N, \bar{K}) > 0, \; Y''(N, \bar{K}) < 0 \tag{5.18}$$

$$ND = ND(W/P, \bar{K}), \; ND'(W/P) < 0 \tag{5.19}$$

$$NS = NS(W/P), \; NS'(W/P) > 0. \tag{5.20}$$

Equations 5.18, 5.19, and 5.20 represent the economy's aggregate production function, labor demand function, and labor supply function, respectively. These functions may be considered as identical (conceptually) to those in the Classical system above. However, in this system in contrast to the Classical framework there is an imperfection in the labor market. In particular, as already noted, the money wage rate is rigid in the downward direction. In other words, institutional forces such as salary contracts, minimum wage laws, labor union contracts, and so forth exist, which prohibit the money wage rate from falling. Thus, given a particular (average) money wage rate in the economy it may be considered as fixed (or rigid) in the short run at least up to full employment. At full employment, however, money wage rates may be considered as entirely flexible upward, as was the case in the Classical system. Thus, we observe that

$$W = \bar{W} \ (\ W \text{ is fixed) for } N < NF \tag{5.21}$$

$$W = \text{flexible upward for } N = NF. \tag{5.22}$$

As in the Classical system, the aggregate price level may be viewed as completely flexible, both upward and downward.[1]

It is convenient for us to express our labor market equilibrium condition in a form quite different from the preceding case. In particular, in this type of economy the level of actual employment (N) is described by

$$N = \min[ND(W/P, \ \bar{K}), NS(W/P)]. \tag{5.23}$$

Equation 5.23 states simply that the actual level of employment in this Keynesian-type labor market is the minimum (lesser) of two quantities: the quantity demanded of labor and the quantity supplied. Henceforth, we shall refer to condition 5.23 as our Keynesian labor market employment condition, not as a labor market equilibrium condition per se. This is because it describes the actual volume of labor employed; however, it does not as such describe an equilibrium, where quantity supplied exactly equals quantity demanded.[2] In any event, it may be helpful to illustrate this labor market employment condition diagrammatically. Refer to figure 5–5, where the real wage is plotted vertically and ND and NS are plotted horizontally. If the real wage were $(W/P)_1$, the quantity supplied of labor (S_1) would exceed the quantity demanded (D_1). However, since the money wage rate is rigid downward, the real wage (in the absence of a price rise) cannot fall. Hence, since employers presumably cannot be forced to hire labor they do not wish to employ, the actual level of employment is D_1 (the quantity of labor demanded). Clearly, the actual level of employment, D_1, is the lesser number of D_1 and S_1. Hence, the actual level of employment is as described in equation 5.23, namely, the minimum of ND and NS.

Consider next the real wage $(W/P)_2$ in figure 5–5. At this real wage the quantity demanded is D^* and the quantity supplied is S^*. Clearly, at such a low real wage rate, $D^* > S^*$. Hence, the actual level of employment would seem to be S^*, the lesser of ND and NS. However, since money wages can rise at full employment, and since at real wage $(W/P)_2$ everyone in the labor force is employed (that is, full employment technically prevails), the excess demand for labor sends the money wage and thus the real wage upward,

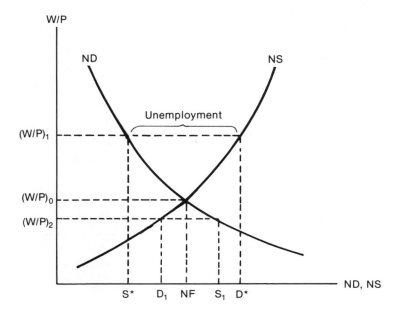

Figure 5–5. Keynesian Labor Market

ultimately to a real wage of $(W/P)_0$.[3] At $(W/P)_0$, $ND = NS$, so that the economy is in equilibrium at full employment (NF). At $(W/P)_0$, the employment level (N) equals both ND and NS. Since NS equals ND at real wage $(W/P)_0$, condition 5.23 is still satisfied.

We may now formally derive the aggregate supply curve for this system. Refer to figure 5–6. In quadrant IV, the production function is represented. In quadrant III, the labor supply and demand functions are plotted. At the intersection of curves NS and ND in quadrant III, the level of employment is given by NF.

Let us assume that the fixed money wage rate is given by $\bar{W}$ in quadrant II. Let us assume that the labor market is initially in full employment equilibrium $(N = NF)$. From the diagram it should be clear that with the real wage ratio at value $(W/P)_0$ and with the money wage rate exactly at value $\bar{W}$, the only price level compatible with full employment, that is, able precisely to yield real wage $(W/P)_0$, is price level $\bar{P}$. In other words, if the price level is value $\bar{P}$ and the money wage rate is $\bar{W}$, we have (at point Z)

$$\left(\frac{W}{P}\right)_0 = \left(\frac{\bar{W}}{\bar{P}}\right). \tag{5.24}$$

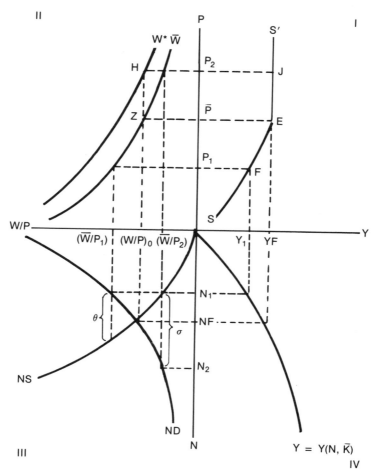

Figure 5–6. Keynesian Supply Curve

Going further, if the money wage rate is $\bar{W}$ and the price level is $\bar{P}$, then the employment level is NF. And, as quadrant IV indicates, if the employment level is NF, the real GNP supplied is YF. Point E in quadrant I, then, with coordinates YF, $\bar{P}$, indicates that the value of real GNP supplied at price level $\bar{P}$ is value YF.

Consider now the impact of a price decrease, say, from $\bar{P}$ to P_1. As the price level falls to P_1, the real wage rises from $(\bar{W}/\bar{P})$ to $(\bar{W}/P_1)$. As this real wage increase occurs the quantity demanded of labor falls and the quantity supplied of labor rises. Hence, at real wage $(\bar{W}/P_1)$, $NS > ND$. This excess supply of labor is shown in quadrant III by distance θ. Thus, since the price level has fallen but the money wage rate is rigid (inflexible) downward, the actual level of employment will be the amount N_1 (since $N_1 < N_2$), where $N_1 = N_2 - \theta$.

Thus, given a money wage rate of $\bar{W}$ and a price level of P_1, the level of employment is given by N_1, where $N_1 < NF$. Moreover, the production function in quadrant IV indicates that an employment level of N_1 will produce a real GNP level of Y_1. Hence, point F in quadrant I, with coordinates Y_1, P_1, indicates that the value of real GNP supplied at price level P_1 is value Y_1.

By considering other price levels below value $\bar{P}$, we can derive other points such as point F along a positively sloped curve that rises up to point E. Like points E and F, these other points would indicate the value of real GNP supplied at particular price levels.

Starting back at point Z, consider next the impact of a price increase, say, from $\bar{P}$ to P_2. As the price level rises to P_2, the real wage falls from $(\bar{W}/\bar{P})$ to $(\bar{W}/P_2)$. As a result, the quantity demanded of labor rises, and the quantity supplied of labor declines. Hence, at real wage $(\bar{W}/P_2)$, $ND > NS$. The amount of this excess demand for labor is shown in quadrant III by distance σ. Now, since everyone who wishes to work at real wage $(\bar{W}/P_2)$ is in fact employed,[4] and since the money wage rate is then flexible upward, the excess demand for labor causes the money wage rate to rise (as employers bid against one another to purchase labor services). As the money wage rate rises, at price level P_2 the real wage rate rises also, thereby lowering the quantity of labor demanded and increasing the quantity of labor supplied. This is illustrated in quadrant III of figure 5–6 by arrows along curves NS and ND. In addition, as the money wage rate is rising, the economy is moving to higher rectangular wage hyperbolas in quadrant II.

The money wage rate continues to rise until the excess demand for labor has disappeared. This will have happened once the full employment real wage $(W/P)_0$ has been reached. Given price level P_2, this occurs at a money wage rate of W^*. The rectangular wage hyperbola corresponding to W^* is shown in quadrant II as running through point H, with coordinates $(W/P)_0$, P_2. Thus, in terms of quadrant II

$$\left(\frac{W}{P}\right)_0 = \left(\frac{W^*}{P_2}\right) = \left(\frac{\bar{W}}{\bar{P}}\right). \tag{5.25}$$

In sum, then, given the price level at P_2 and the full employment wage at W^*, the employment level is NF. Furthermore, if the employment level is NF, the level of real GNP produced is YF. Point J in quadrant I, with coordinates YF, P_2, thus indicates that the value of real GNP supplied at price level P_2 would be YF.

If we start back at point Z with $\bar{P}$ and postulate other price increases, we can derive other points such as E and J in quadrant I. As should be quite clear, all such points would lie along a vertical line rising from point E.

In conclusion, then, in this Keynesian-type labor market, the aggregate supply curve has two distinct portions: a positively sloped section up to the full employment level of real GNP and a vertical section then beginning at the full employment real GNP level. This exemplified by the curve SES' in quadrant I of figure 5–6.

Aggregate Demand Curve

The aggregate demand curve can be easily derived by simply integrating the analyses in chapters 2 and 3. The derivation of the aggregate demand curve, in the simplest case, hinges on the fact that a price change alters the real money supply and thereby shifts the LM curve. Moreover, the technique developed below can be modified to address more complex forms of economic behavior.

Derivation

In order to derive the aggregate demand curve, we shall consider the following familiar forms of economic behavior:

$$Y = C + I + G + X + R \tag{5.25}$$

$$C = C(Yd, i) \tag{5.27}$$

$$I = I(Y, i) \tag{5.28}$$

$$G = \bar{G} \tag{5.29}$$

$$T = \bar{T} \tag{5.30}$$

$$X = \bar{X} \tag{5.31}$$

$$R = \bar{R} + R(Y) \tag{5.32}$$

$$Ms/P = Md \tag{5.33}$$

$$Md = Md(Y, i) \tag{5.34}$$

$$Ms = \bar{M} \tag{5.35}$$

where it is arbitrarily assumed that

$$\frac{\partial S}{\partial Yd} > \frac{\partial I}{\partial Y} \tag{5.36}$$

Figure 5–7 consists of two panels. The upper panel provides the familiar mapping of real GNP and the interest rate. The lower panel plots real GNP along the abscissa and the aggregate price level on the ordinate axis. Start at point A in the upper panel. Point A, with coordinates (Yo, io), is the equilibrium between curves IS and LM for $P = Po$, as illustrated by the notation along the LM curve. At point A, given price level Po, the economy demands Yo worth of real GNP. The real GNP of Yo demanded at price Po is shown at point A' in the lower panel.

Now let the price level fall to $\bar{P}$. The LM curve shifts down and a new equilibrium at point B is established. At point B, the real GNP demanded at price level $\bar{P}$ is $\bar{Y}$. These two data are then recorded in the lower panel at point B'. Connecting points A' and B', as well as other such points similarly derived, yield the aggregate demand curve (DD) in the lower panel of figure 5–7.

Other Considerations

It is left to the reader to derive demand curves for other economic systems. It should be noted that if the IS curve is perfectly vertical[5] the aggregate demand curve will also be perfectly vertical. Conversely, if the LM curve is perfectly vertical,[6] while the IS curve is negatively sloped, the aggregate demand curve remains negatively sloped (given the conventional stability condition).

Naturally, in the derivation in figure 5–7, the discretionary monetary and fiscal policies of the system were unchanged. The reader can use the apparatus in figure 5–7 to verify the following general arguments. Given a positively sloped LM curve and the stability condition requiring the slope of the LM curve to algebraically exceed the slope of the IS curve, then (1) an expansionary monetary policy shifts the demand curve rightward, and (2) an expansionary fiscal policy shifts the demand curve rightward.

Macroeconomic Policy

In this final section of the chapter we examine the workings of the complete system. We shall focus principally on the Keynesian system; however, observations regarding the Classical system will be provided as well. Our procedure will be, following the pattern in chapter 4, to first consider monetary policy and then, separately, to consider fiscal policy.

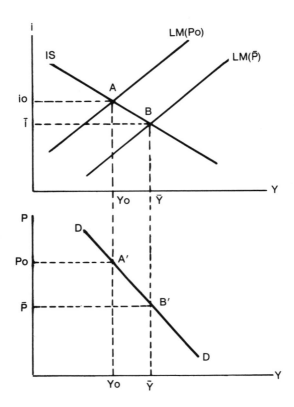

Figure 5–7. Aggregate Demand

Monetary Policy

Let us consider the Keynesian labor market developed in the first section of this chapter. In addition, let us consider the commodity and money markets summarized in equations 5.26 through 5.36. Figure 5–8 illustrates a general IS-LM equilibrium in the economy at $Y = Yo$, $i = io$, and $P = Po$, where $Yo < YF$ and Yo corresponds to an employment level of No, where $No < NF$. The IS curve initially crosses curve $\text{LM}(Po)'$ at point A.

Let us examine the impact of an expansionary monetary policy. Such a policy shifts the LM curve to, say, $\text{LM}(Po)''$ This lowers the interest rate (to $\bar{i}$) and results in a higher real GNP demanded, $\bar{Y}$. This corresponds to point B in the upper panel of figure 5–8. Meanwhile, the expansionary monetary policy has shifted the aggregate demand schedule to $D'D'$, so that there is excess demand at price level Po. Excess demand pushes up the aggregate price level until equilibrium is established at coordinates (Y^*, P^*) in the lower

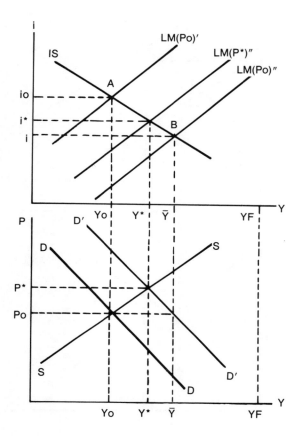

Figure 5–8. Monetary Policy

Meanwhile, the higher price level has shifted the LM curve leftward to LM(P^*)″, corresponding to real GNP level Y^* i the upper panel.

In the end, then, the expansionary monetary policy has raised the real GNP level by ($Y^* - Yo$), raised the price level by ($P^* - Po$), and reduced the interest rate by ($io - i^*$). Thus, the expansionary monetary policy has combatted recession by elevating production and employment but caused prices to increase. A contractionary monetary policy would, in principle, work in the opposite fashion.

Fiscal Policy

Let us refer next to figure 5–9 and examine fiscal policy. As in figure 5–8, we begin in equilibrium at $Y = Yo$, $i = io$, and $P = Po$, where $Yo < YF$ and Yo

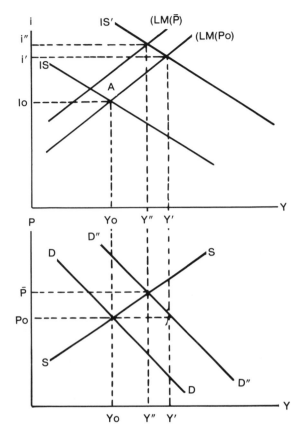

Figure 5–9. Fiscal Policy

corresponds to *No,* where *No* < *NF.* The curve IS initially crosses curve LM (*Po*) at point A.

Consider the impact of an expansionary fiscal policy. Such a policy shifts the IS curve from IS to, say, IS′. This pushes the economy toward demanding a higher real GNP level at price level *Po,* namely, *Y′.* The fiscal policy also shifts the aggregate demand curve from *DD* to *D″D″,* so that at price level *Po* there is excess demand. Excess demand drives up the aggregate price level toward an equilibrium value of $\bar{P}$ that corresponds to $Y = Y''$. With a higher price level, the LM curve shifts leftward until the system is fully equilibrated in the money and commodity markets in a manner consistent with $P = \bar{P}$ and $Y = Y''$.

Thus, an expansionary fiscal policy acts to raise the real GNP level by

$(Y'' - Yo)$, raise the price level by $(\bar{P} - Po)$, and raise the interest rate $(i'' - io)$. Once again, we observe that an expansionary economic policy acts not only to raise production and employment, but prices as well. A contractionary fiscal policy would tend to have the opposite impacts.

We close with a remark about the crude Classical system. As already noted, the crude Classical system is characterized by a perfectly vertical aggregate supply curve corresponding to full employment equilibrium. Hence, when the system is in equilibrium it is also at full employment.[7] Using the vertical supply curve it can be easily shown that (1) raising the nominal money supply raises the price level (the so-called crude quantity theory of money), not the real GNP level; and (2) changing fiscal policy changes the interest rate but not the real GNP level.[8]

Notes

1. To be sure, one may argue that there is often price rigidity (especially downward) in the real world.

2. This condition of labor employment can of course also be stated as $W/P = Y'(N, \bar{K})$.

3. It should be pointed out that, although full employment technically prevails at real wage $(W/P)_2$, this is *not* full employment equilibrium. This is evident from the fact that the quantity supplied of labor at $(W/P)_2$ does not equal the quantity demanded of labor.

4. Thus, while full employment equilibrium does not exist, full employment does.

5. This outcome might be the result of the commodity market's not being interest sensitive, that is, $\partial C/\partial i = \partial I/\partial i = 0$.

6. This would occur if $\partial Md/\partial i = 0$.

7. In the crude Classical system, the LM curve is perfectly vertical.

8. Good reference material for this chapter is given by Keynes (1936) and Patinkin (1948, 1965).

References

Keynes, J.M., 1936. *The General Theory of Employment, Interest and Money,* New York: Harcourt, Brace and Company.

Patinkin, D., 1948. Price Flexibility and Full Employment, *American Economic Review,* vol. 38, pp. 543–564.

Patinkin, D., 1965. *Money, Interest and Prices,* 2nd ed. New York: Harper and Row.

III
Core Analysis

III
Ore Analysis

6
Crowding Out and Fiscal Policy

Much of the current debate in the United States about the effects of our large federal budget deficits (past, present, and projected) centers around the allegedly adverse economic impact of such deficits. In turn, the adverse economic impact of budget deficits is probably most frequently associated with the phenomenon known as crowding out, although the inflationary impact of deficits has received considerable attention in recent years (see, for example, Dwyer, 1982).

Crowding out, in general, refers to the effects of expansionary fiscal actions on private sector spending (principally, private investment and consumption outlays). As Carlson and Spencer (1975, p. 3) have observed "if an increase in government demand ($\Delta G > 0$), financed by either taxes or debt issuance to the public, fails to stimulate total economic activity, the private sector is . . . "crowded out" by the government action." In perhaps its simplest form, crowding out refers to the offsetting changes in private investment and consumption outlays resulting when an expansionary fiscal action acts to raise the interest rate. As will be demonstrated below, however, the means by which private investment and consumption may be crowded out by the expansionary fiscal policy can be rather complex.

This chapter summarizes and analyzes the topic of crowding out at the analytical level. We begin here with a brief description of crowding out. Next, we proceed to examine various theories or interpretations of crowding out. This material will serve as a useful backdrop for the empirical analyses provided in chapters 7, 8, and 9.

Crowding Out: General Observations

As already noted, crowding out implies that increased government spending displaces private sector spending. Let ΔG represent increased government spending and let ΔZ represent decreased private sector spending. Utilizing this notation, we may classify crowding out in three different ways. To start, if

$$|\Delta G| = |\Delta Z|, \tag{6.1}$$

then the degree of crowding out is said to be complete. On the other hand, if

$$|\Delta G| > |\Delta Z|, \tag{6.2}$$

then partial crowding out is said to occur. Finally, if

$$|\Delta G| > |\Delta Z| = 0, \tag{6.3}$$

then zero crowding out is said to exist.

At the empirical level, the possibility that crowding out may be complete can be traced to the studies by Anderson and Jordan (1968) and Keran (1969, 1970). Other empirical studies, such as Abrams and Schmitz (1978), Arestis (1979), Zahn (1978), and Cebula, Carlos, and Koch (1981), have found evidence of only partial crowding out. Still other studies, such as Hoelscher (1983) and Evans (1985), suggest that crowding out may be statistically unimportant. These empirical studies use different techniques, examine different variables, and consider different time periods. Thus, the fact that they generate varying results should come as no surprise. In part, the fact that these results differ so much is traceable to the fact that some empirical (as well as some theoretical) analyses examine the crowding out impact of government spending, whereas other studies examine the crowding out impact of government budget deficits. Although these two phenomena are obviously closely related, they clearly are not synonymous. Accordingly, in the analysis below, as well as in chapter 7, we shall distinguish between the crowding out effect of government spending increases and the crowding out effect of government budget deficits.

Crowding Out in the Crude Classical System

The basic elements of the crude Classical system are lucidly developed by Patinkin (1948, 1965). To demonstrate the crowding out phenomenon in the crude Classical system, the following system of equations is to be considered:

$$Y = C + I + G \tag{6.4}$$

$$C = C(Yd, i) \tag{6.5}$$

$$I = I(Y, i) \tag{6.6}$$

$$G = \bar{G} \tag{6.7}$$

$$T = \bar{T} \tag{6.8}$$

$$Ms/P = Md \qquad\qquad (6.9)$$

$$Md = Md(Y) \qquad\qquad (6.10)$$

$$Ms = \bar{M} \qquad\qquad (6.11)$$

$$Y = Y(N, \bar{K}) \qquad\qquad (6.12)$$

$$ND = ND(W/P) \qquad\qquad (6.13)$$

$$NS = NS(W/P) \qquad\qquad (6.14)$$

$$W, P = \text{perfectly flexible} \qquad\qquad (6.15)$$

$$NS = ND, \qquad\qquad (6.16)$$

where it is also assumed that

$$\frac{\partial S}{\partial Yd} > \frac{\partial I}{\partial Y}. \qquad\qquad (6.17)$$

The system shown in equations 6.4 through 6.17 is one possible inter-pretation of the crude Classical system. For example, it is not uncommon for the interest rate to be omitted from the consumption function or for the GNP level to be omitted from the investment function in the crude Classical sys-tem. Nevertheless, the outcomes and critical traits of the system conform to the norm (see, for example, Patinkin, 1948, 1965). Next we observe that, as noted in chapter 2, condition 6.17 is sufficient in this system to generate a negatively sloped IS curve. Moreover, the fact that money demand does not depend on the interest rate implies a vertical LM curve (see chapter 3). Finally, the labor market in this system, since it is characterized by perfect flexibility of both money wages (W) and prices (P), generates a perfectly vertical aggre-gate supply curve (see chapter 5).

Figure 6–1 shows the economy to be initially in equilibrium at interest rate i' and real GNP level YF, given $G = \bar{G}$ and $T = \bar{T}$, and hence IS curve IS'. If the level of government spending is to be increased, we must somehow finance the spending increase. This notion may be easily described with the use of a government budget constraint. Essentially, a *government budget constraint* describes the relationship between the level of government spend-ing and the sources of funds required to finance that spending. One possible form of a government budget constraint is shown by:

$$G - T = \Delta Ms + \Delta B, \qquad\qquad (6.18)$$

where ΔB represents bond sales by the Treasury to the public to help finance

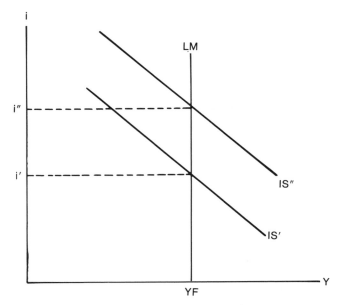

Figure 6–1. Classical Crowding Out

$(G - T)$. In order to describe the crowding out effect of fiscal policy, it is appropriate here to hold

$$\Delta Ms = 0. \tag{6.19}$$

Hence, equation 6.18 becomes

$$G - T = \Delta B. \tag{6.20}$$

To simplify matters further, we demonstrate crowding out in the crude Classical system by holding

$$\Delta T = 0. \tag{6.21}$$

Accordingly, if we increase government spending by ΔG, then

$$\Delta G = \Delta B. \tag{6.22}$$

In terms of figure 6–1, this bond-financed fiscal policy has the effect of shifting the IS curve from IS' to IS". Clearly, the new IS-LM equilibrium corresponds to the higher interest rate i'' and the unchanged real GNP level YF. Hence, in this crude Classical system, crowding out is said to be complete. That is, it follows that

$$|\Delta G| = |\Delta C| + |\Delta I|. \tag{6.23}$$

As the Treasury sold new bonds to finance ΔG, the interest rate in the economy was pushed upward. In turn, the levels of C and I were both reduced. Since the equilibrium real GNP level was left unchanged, government spending crowded out private sector spending dollar-for-dollar. Moreover, the fiscal policy action simply redistributed GNP from the private sector of the economy to the public sector of the economy.

Crowding Out in the Crude Keynesian Model

The so-called crude Keynesian system may be described by the following:

$$Y = C + I + G \tag{6.24}$$

$$C = C(Yd) \tag{6.25}$$

$$I = \bar{I} \tag{6.26}$$

$$G = \bar{G} \tag{6.27}$$

$$T = \bar{T} \tag{6.28}$$

$$Ms/P = Md \tag{6.29}$$

$$Md = Md(Y, i) \tag{6.30}$$

$$Ms = \bar{M} \tag{6.31}$$

$$Y = Y(N, \bar{K}) \tag{6.32}$$

$$ND = ND(W/P) \tag{6.33}$$

$$NS = NS(W/P) \tag{6.34}$$

$$W = \text{rigid downward} \tag{6.35}$$

$$W = \text{flexible upward at full employment} \tag{6.36}$$

$$P = \text{flexible upward and downward} \tag{6.37}$$

$$N = \min [ND, NS]. \tag{6.38}$$

The system summarized in equations 6.24 through 6.38 represents an extreme interpretation of the macromodel in *The General Theory of Employment, Interest, and Money* by John M. Keynes (1936).

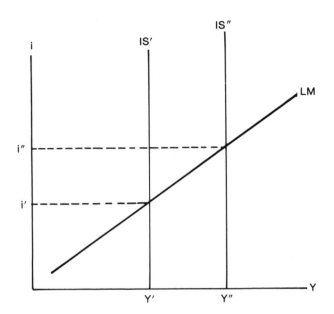

Figure 6–2. Crude Keynesian Case

In the system shown above the IS curve is perfectly vertical due to the absence of an interest rate effect in the commodity market. The LM curve, however, unlike that in the crude Classical system, is positively sloped. Moreover, the aggregate supply schedule is upward sloping to the point of full employment (*YF*) and then perfectly vertical above that point as shown in figure 5–6 (in chapter 5).

Figure 6–2 illustrates the economy at an initial IS-LM equilibrium at interest rate i' and real GNP level Y', given $G = \bar{G}$, $T = \bar{T}$, and hence IS curve IS′. If the government spending level is increased and solely financed by Treasury bond sales to the public, then the IS curve shifts rightward to IS″. The economy then moves to real GNP level Y'' and interest rate i''. Notice that, given the interest insensitivity of commodity market demand, the higher interest rate resulting from the policy cannot affect (that is, reduce) private sector spending. In this system private sector spending is simply not crowded out at all by the expansionary fiscal policy. The reader can readily demonstrate that, even if we allow for the effects of a rising aggregate price level on the LM curve (see chapters 3 and 5), the crude Keynesian case is associated with zero crowding out. This is because as the price level increases and the LM curve then shifts upward, the IS-LM equilibrium still corresponds to the same, new real GNP level, namely, real GNP Y''.

Keynes and Public Expectations

The previous section of this chapter sketches out a scenario wherein the crude Keynesian system generates zero crowding out. In this section a more moderate version of Keynesian system is considered, one that allows for a marginal efficiency of capital (see chapter 2) and public confidence and expectations.

Keynes (1936, p. 120) was somewhat concerned that government spending could adversely affect public confidence. In turn, the effect of the government spending program was seen as potentially increasing liquidity preference (*Md*) and decreasing the marginal efficiency of capital. To illustrate these possible impacts from a government spending program, we focus on figure 6–3, where the IS curve is depicted as negatively sloped and where the LM curve is shown to be positively sloped.[1]

The economy is shown initially in figure 6–3 to be in equilibrium at the intersection of curves LM and IS′, where, given $G = \bar{G}$, the interest rate is i' and the real GNP level is Y'. Now let G rise by ΔG to the level $\bar{G} + \Delta G$. This shifts the IS curve from IS′ to IS″ and generates a new IS-LM equilibrium at $Y = Y''$ and $i = i''$. However, as a result of the rising government spending level, liquidity preference is increased, shifting the LM curve to the left; and the marginal efficiency of capital is decreased, shifting the IS curve to the left as well.

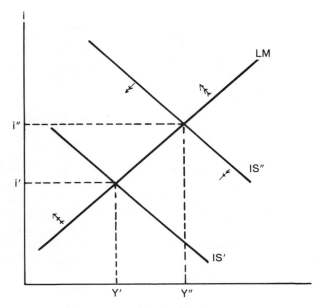

Figure 6–3. Second Keynesian Case

Clearly, as the LM and IS curves both shift to the left, the real GNP level is being reduced below Y''. Depending on the relative shifts of the LM and IS curve, the degree of crowding out could theoretically be either partial or complete.[2] Clearly, the results shown in figure 6–3 differ sharply from those in figure 6–2.

Transactions Crowding Out

Perhaps the simplest and best known form of crowding out is that known as *transactions crowding out*. We may examine this concept with the use of the following commodity market:

$$Y = C + I + G \tag{6.39}$$

$$C = C(Yd, i) = a + bYd - ei \tag{6.40}$$

$$I = I(Y, i) = \bar{I} + fY - hi \tag{6.41}$$

$$G = \bar{G} \tag{6.42}$$

$$T = \bar{T}. \tag{6.43}$$

The equilibrium GNP in this market is given by

$$Y = \frac{a - b\bar{T} - ei + \bar{I} - hi + \bar{G}}{1 - b - f}. \tag{6.44}$$

The simple government spending multiplier corresponding to system 6.39–6.43, $\Delta Y/\Delta G$, is given by

$$\frac{\Delta Y}{\Delta G} = \frac{1}{1 - b - f}. \tag{6.45}$$

The money market is given by equations 6.29, 6.30, and 6.31, whereas the labor market is given by equations 6.32 through 6.38.

Refer now to figure 6–4, where the economy is shown to be initially in equilibrium at interest rate i^* and real GNP level Y^*, that is, at the intersection of curves IS* and LM*. The level of government spending along IS* is given by $\bar{G}$. Now let the government spending level rise by the amount ΔG. Let us assume that this increased government spending is financed solely by Treasury bond sales to the public:

$$\Delta G = \Delta B. \tag{6.46}$$

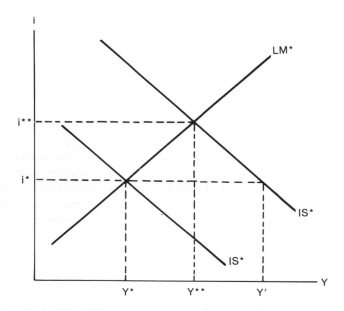

Figure 6–4. Simple Transactions Crowding Out

The rise in government spending shifts the IS curve rightward to IS**; specifically, the IS curve is shifted rightward by the amount

$$\Delta G \left(\frac{1}{1 - b - f} \right) \tag{6.47}$$

However, whereas the IS curve shifts rightward by this amount, the level of GNP cannot rise by as much as this amount. This is because as the level of GNP begins to increase, the aggregate demand for money also increases. In turn, a rising aggregate demand for money elevates the interest rate and, in so doing, reduces both investment and consumption. Thus, due to the expansion brought on by $\Delta G (\Delta G > 0)$, the transactions demand for money is increased, which in turn raises interest rates and thereby discourages investment and consumption as the economy moves along curve LM* from coordinates Y^*, i^* to coordinates Y^{**}, i^{**}.[3]

The change in GNP that would have occurred as a result of ΔG in the absence of transactions crowding out is given by

$$Y' - Y^*. \tag{6.48}$$

The actual change in GNP that occurs is given by

$$Y^{**} - Y^*. \tag{6.49}$$

Hence, transactions crowding out results in partial crowding out in the amount of

$$Y' - Y^{**} = (Y' - Y^*) - (Y^{**} - Y^*). \tag{6.50}$$

In closing this section, it is clear that the extent of the partial crowding out resulting from transactions crowding out depends significantly on the relative slopes of the IS and LM curves. The interested reader is referred to the theoretical paper by Meyer (1983) and to the empirical study by Sullivan (1976). The latter actually provides an empirical estimate of the slopes of these two curves.

Ultrarationality

Yet another theory of crowding out has been formulated by David and Scadding (1974). David and Scadding assume *ultrarationality* on the part of households. Households are portrayed as viewing the government sector and the corporate sector of the economy as, in effect, extensions of themselves, that is, as vehicles for the pursuit of their private interests. Accordingly, a government budget deficit presumably displaces an equal amount of private investment because deficit financing is interpreted as public investment. Deficit financing is therefore a substitute for private investment since households regard private investment and public investment as merely alternative means of achieving an increased flow of future consumption benefits.

Ultrarationality may be illustrated in part by figure 6–5. The economy is shown initially to be in equilibrium at the intersection of curves IS' and LM, corresponding to real GNP level Y' and interest rate i'. Let government spending rise by ΔG, which amount is financed by borrowing from the public:

$$\Delta G = \Delta B. \tag{6.51}$$

This policy initially shifts the IS curve rightward from IS' to IS". However, the equal decline in private investment shifts the IS curve leftward from IS" back to IS'. Thus, as we have seen elsewhere, the implication is complete crowding out.

It should be noted that this same final conclusion, namely, that of complete crowding out due to ultrarationality, is obtained if the increased government spending is financed through taxes on households. In such a case, the

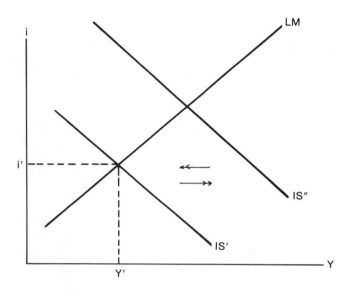

Figure 6–5. Ultrarationality

tax-financed expenditure increase presumably displaces private consumption outlays because the expenditure increase is evaluated in terms of its current consumption benefits and will be simply substituted by households for private consumer outlays.

Whether the increased government expenditure is financed through bond sales to the public or through increased taxes on households, the outcome is the same: complete crowding out. The ultimate impact of the policy will be to merely redistribute the economy's output from the private sector (corporate or household) of the economy to the government sector of the economy. Actually, as shown above, this final outcome is somewhat similar to that obtained in the crude Classical system, except that the mechanism in the present case is ultrarationality, whereas the mechanism is the interest rate (at full employment) in the crude Classical case.[4]

Two brief comments may now be in order. First, one might wish to question the underlying tenet of ultrarationality, that is, the perfect substitution in the eyes of the household sector of, say, public investment for private investment. Second, if there were only a limited degree of substitution of public investment for private investment, then a so-modified form of ultrarationality might conceivably be inferred as leading to only partial crowding out.

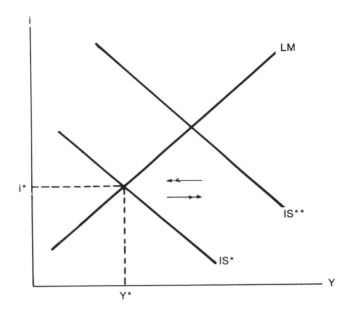

Figure 6–6. Financial Crowding Out

Financial Crowding Out

Financial crowding out is sometimes confused with *transactions crowding out.* [5] This confusion may stem from the role that the interest rate, an obvious category of financial variable, plays in transactions crowding out. As illustrated below, however, financial crowding out is quite different.

In order to illustrate financial crowding out we refer to figure 6–6, where the economy is shown to be initially in equilibrium at the intersection of curves IS* and LM, where the interest rate is i^* and the real GNP level is Y^*. Let the level of government spending rise by ΔG; furthermore, let ΔG be financed by Treasury bond sales to the public. The increased government spending level shifts the IS curve from IS* to IS**. Nobel laureate Milton Friedman (1970, 1971), and other economists as well, have argued that this shift in the IS curve is only temporary, however.

More specifically, according to the financial crowding out hypothesis, investment presumably depends not only on the interest rate, but also on the supply of savings available for firms to borrow for investment purposes, F.

Thus, we have

$$I = I(i, F), \tag{6.52}$$

where

$$\frac{\partial I}{\partial i} < 0, \frac{\partial I}{\partial F} > 0. \tag{6.53}$$

If government spending rises by ΔG and if the increased spending is solely financed by bond sales to the public so that[6]

$$\Delta G = \Delta B, \tag{6.54}$$

then it may be argued that the deficit (ΔB) absorbs ΔG worth of savings (F) that would have otherwise presumably been funneled to firms for private investment. Accordingly, it is argued that private investment spending declines by an amount equal in absolute value to $\Delta G = \Delta B$:

$$|\Delta I| = |\Delta G| = |\Delta B|. \tag{6.55}$$

This sequence of events in turn allegedly implies that the IS curve will then shift leftward from IS** back to IS*. Consequently, the degree of the crowding out is complete, and the value of the government spending multiplier (dY/dG) is zero. As we have seen elsewhere,[7] the net final impact of the fiscal action is not to alter the final real GNP level, but rather merely to alter the composition of real GNP, with investment in this case simply being replaced, dollar-for-dollar, by government spending.

Portfolio Crowding Out and the Wealth Effect

Yet another theory of crowding out involves *portfolio crowding out* and real net wealth effects. There are many economists including Patinkin (1965), who argue that the private sector demand for both commodities and money is influenced, in part, by household real net worth. Consider, for example, the following two simple relationships:

$$C = C(Yd, i, W^H) \tag{6.56}$$

$$Md = Md(Y, i, W^H), \tag{6.57}$$

where W^H equals household real net wealth and where

$$1 > \frac{\partial C}{\partial Yd} > 0, \frac{\partial C}{\partial i} < 0, \frac{\partial C}{\partial W^H} > 0 \qquad (6.58)$$

$$\frac{\partial Md}{\partial Y} > 0, \frac{\partial Md}{\partial i} < 0, \frac{\partial Md}{\partial W^H} > 0. \qquad (6.59)$$

Given the behavior described in equations 6.56 through 6.59, we may proceed to examine a simple form of portfolio crowding out.

Refer now to figure 6–7, where the economy is initially shown to be in equilibrium at the intersection of curves IS′ and LM′, corresponding to real GNP level Y' and interest rate i'. The curve IS′ is predicated on the government spending level $\bar{G}$. Now let government spending rise by ΔG, and let ΔG be financed solely by sales of bonds to the public. The initial impact of this fiscal policy action of course is to shift the IS curve to the right, say, to IS″. This outcome gives the initial impression of a rise in the interest rate (to i'') and a rise in the real GNP level (to Y'') as well. Thus, at the end of period 1, it seems that $\Delta i > 0$ and $\Delta Y > 0$, as a result of the fiscal action. Of course, the effects of the fiscal action in question at this point reflect a partial transacactions crowding out to the extent of $Y^* - Y''$ in figure 6–7.

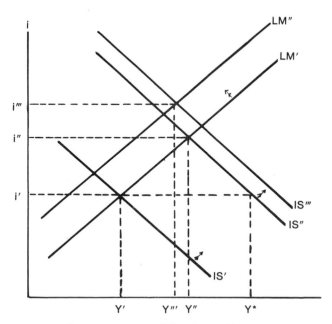

Figure 6–7. Portfolio Crowding out

Whatever bonds the government sells to finance its first(initial)-period deficit have no impact on C or Md until the next time period (or period 2). In other words, if the government sells bonds to the public to finance a first-period deficit ($= \Delta G$), these same bonds will become a part of households' real net wealth at the beginning of the next (second) time period.

In any event, it is apparent that at some point the household sector's real net wealth rises due to the increase in the household sector's holdings of government bonds. This in turn has two effects on the economy: (1) it raises consumption spending and thereby shifts the IS curve to the right (upward); and (2) it raises money demand (real) and thereby shifts the LM curve to the left (upward). On the one hand, the impact of the IS curve shift is to raise the GNP level (and interest rates as well, of course). On the other hand, the impact of the LM curve shift is to lower the GNP level (while pushing interest rates upward).

Whether the LM curve will shift to the left more than the IS curve will shift to the right is not known on a priori grounds. One theoretically possible outcome from the described shifting of these two curves is illustrated in figure 6–7, where the IS curve is shown to have shifted from IS″ to IS‴ and where the LM curve is shown to have shifted from LM′ to LM″. Given curves IS‴ and LM″, the economy is shown to be in equilibrium at real GNP level Y''' and interest rate i'''.

Thus, as shown in figure 6–7, it would appear that wealth effects such as those shown in equations 6.56 through 6.59 might potentially lead to partial portfolio crowding out. Nevertheless, the net effect of the fiscal action in question (where $\Delta G = \Delta B$), in the context of the wealth effect, is still ambiguous.[8,9]

Portfolio Substitution Crowding Out

Klein (1972) has provided another possible source (form) of crowding out. It is referred to as portfolio substitution crowding out. This hypothesis essentially argues that new government bond issues, because of their substitutability for commodities and money, affect the locations of both IS and LM curves and hence may significantly alter the effectiveness of fiscal policy actions on the economy.

Refer to figure 6–8, where the economy is initially in equilibrium at the intersection of curves IS* and LM*, corresponding to real GNP level Y^* and interest rate i^*. We begin by increasing the government spending level by ΔG and by financing the spending increase by a sale of new government bonds to, say, the nonbank public. This has the initial impact of shifting the IS curve rightward from IS* to IS**. In turn, the economy appears to move from real

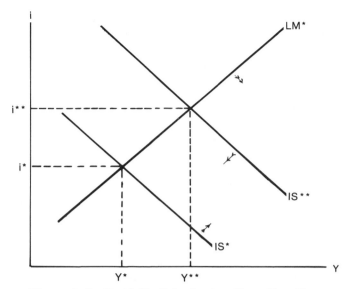

Figure 6–8. Portfolio Substitution Crowding Out

GNP level Y^* to real GNP level Y^{**} and from interest rate i^* to interest rate i^{**}. Hence, the initial impacts of the policy appear to be

$$\Delta Y > 0, \Delta i > 0. \tag{6.60}$$

Naturally, in moving from coordinates Y^*, i^* to coordinates Y^{**}, i^{**}, the economy experiences partial transactions crowding out (see figure 6–4).

Let us now consider the alleged effects of ΔB according to Klein (1972). Klein (1972) argues that the nonbank public, after the government has borrowed the funds required to finance the deficit and after the government has spent those funds, has as much money as before. However, it also has additional (and new) government bonds. As these new bonds were being issued to the nonbank public they were competing with commodities and money for a place in the portfolios of the nonbank public. The successful sale of the newly issued government bonds implies a substitution of these new bonds for commodities and money. Hence, the demand for commodities presumably must decline, as must the demand for money. In turn, this fact implies a leftward shifting of the IS curve and a rightward shifting of the LM curve. Klein argues that if the new IS-LM equilibrium lies to the left of real GNP level Y^{**} in figure 6–8 (and it may or may not), then partial crowding out (of the portfolio substitution variety) occurs. This is, of course, in addition to the obvious transactions crowding out (partial) that also occurs.

Klein (1972) also examines wealth effects in his analysis. When he integrates wealth effects with his substitution crowding out hypothesis, he derives nine different possible combinations of net shifts in the IS and LM curves being generated by an expansionary, bond-financed fiscal action. He does not evaluate the relative likelihoods of these nine possible outcomes; that is, he does not indicate which outcomes are less likely to occur or which are more likely to occur. Nor does he examine the stability implications of these various possible alternatives. However, several of the outcome possibilities are shown to be compatible with a partial crowding out effect.

Negative Transactions Crowding Out

It is commonplace in conventional macroeconomic models to assume that consumption and/or investment is inversely related to the interest rate. However, a number of empirical studies such as Izenson (1983), Weber (1970, 1975), and Yarrow (1975) have cast at least some doubt on the validity of these two very familiar assumptions. Moreover, without accepting or rejecting the validity of these empirical findings (especially Weber, 1970, 1975, and Yarrow, 1975), Cebula (1976) has examined some of the potential implications of the findings for public policy effectiveness. The findings by Cebula (1976) have been extended somewhat by Wang (1980), Cebula (1980), and Hwang and Yu (1984). Nevertheless, no one has as yet expressly addressed the implications of the various empirical findings in Weber (1970, 1975), Yarrow (1975), and Izenson (1983) for the issue of crowding out. Such an analysis is to be provided below, however.

Weber (1970, 1975) has empirically examined the responsiveness of consumption expenditures to changes in the interest rate. His empirical results imply that consumption expenditures are (on balance) directly a function of the interest rate. As Weber (1970, p. 600) observes, "When the rate of interest increases, consumers have the opportunity to maintain the same level of consumption in the future with less saving today. Consequently, they increase current consumption in response to the interest rate increase." Moreover, the second study by Weber (1975) generates the same essential conclusion; in particular, Weber (1975, p. 857) has found that "an increase in the weighted average of current and past nominal interest rates would increase consumer expenditures on both nondurables and durables. This finding is in accord with . . . my earlier study of consumption."

In an altogether separate vein, Yarrow (1975, p. 582) has argued that "the growth rate of the firm, and hence its level of investment, may be an *increasing* function of the rate of interest . . . Such behavior is said to be a characteristic of the growth-maximizing firm (as opposed to the profit-maximizing firm). Yarrow's (1975) analysis is both theoretical and empirical in nature.

Moreover, the study by Izenson (1983) offers empirical support for the notion that investment is an increasing function of the interest rate. Izenson (1983) examines three different regressions. In all three cases, Izenson (1983, p. 137) finds that "The coefficient on the interest rate variable (INR) is positive and significant far beyond the 0.01 level; this strongly confirms Yarrow's suspicions that the rate of investment might be positively linked with the rate of interest, for the growth maximizing firm."

Without rejecting or accepting the findings in Weber (1970, 1975), Yarrow (1975), and Izenson (1983) as either valid or invalid, this section of the chapter examines the theoretical implications of these findings for the crowding out issue. The analysis that follows generates what is to be referred to here as negative transactions crowding out.

The basic model is given by

$$Y = C + I + G \tag{6.61}$$

$$C = C(Yd, i) \tag{6.62}$$

$$I = I(Y, i) \tag{6.63}$$

$$G = \bar{G} \tag{6.64}$$

$$T = \bar{T} \tag{6.65}$$

$$Ms/P = Md \tag{6.66}$$

$$Ms = \bar{M} \tag{6.67}$$

$$Md = Md(Y, i). \tag{6.68}$$

As we have been doing, we ignore, for simplicity, variations in the aggregate price level. While the economy summarized in equations 6.61 through 6.68 is a closed system, the analysis can be easily applied to the case of an open system as well. Indeed, we shall briefly do so later on in this section of the chapter.

In accord with Weber (1970, 1975), it is assumed here that

$$\frac{\partial C}{\partial i} > 0. \tag{6.69}$$

In accord with the aforementioned studies by Yarrow (1975) and Izenson (1983), it is also assumed here that

$$\frac{\partial I}{\partial i} > 0. \tag{6.70}$$

The remaining restrictions on the partial derivatives in the system are, as follows:

$$1 > \frac{\partial C}{\partial Yd} > 0 \qquad (6.71)$$

$$1 > \frac{\partial I}{\partial Y} > 0 \qquad (6.72)$$

$$\frac{\partial Md}{\partial Y} > 0, \frac{\partial Md}{\partial i} < 0. \qquad (6.73)$$

Hereafter, we follow earlier chapters and let subscripted terms denote partial differentiation. Accordingly, the slope of the IS curve is then given by

$$\frac{(I - C_Y - I_Y)}{(C_i + I_i)} . \qquad (6.74)$$

In addition, the slope of the LM curve, given $dp = 0$, is then given by

$$-\frac{Md_Y}{Md_i} > 0. \qquad (6.75)$$

Given the system in equations 6.61 through 6.73, it is now necessary to derive the condition for IS-LM stability. We shall herein utilize the technique demonstrated in chapter 4. We begin by taking the total differentials of the following two summary equations:

$$Y = C(Yd, i) + I(Y, i) + G \qquad (6.76)$$

$$\bar{M}/P = Md(Y, i), \qquad (6.77)$$

where, by definition, we have

$$Yd = Y - \bar{T} \qquad (6.78)$$

and where

$$dP = 0 \qquad (6.79)$$

by assumption (merely to simplify the analysis).

The total differentials of equations 6.76 and 6.77 are, respectively, given by equations 6.80 and 6.81:

$$dY = C_Y dY + C_i di + I_Y dY + I_i di + dG \tag{6.80}$$

$$d\bar{M} = Md_Y dY + Md_i di. \tag{6.81}$$

Rearranging the terms in equations 6.80 and 6.81 yields, respectively, equations 6.82 and 6.83:

$$-d\bar{G} = (C_Y + I_Y - 1)dY + (C_i + I_i)di \tag{6.82}$$

$$d\bar{M} = Md_Y dY + Md_i di. \tag{6.83}$$

The Routh-Hurwitz stability condition requires that

$$\begin{vmatrix} (C_Y + I_Y - 1) & (C_i + I_i) \\ Md_Y & Md_i \end{vmatrix} > 0. \tag{6.84}$$

The expanded determinant is given by

$$(C_Y + I_Y - 1)(Md_i) - (C_i + I_i)(Md_Y) > 0. \tag{6.85}$$

Multiplying through by -1 yields

$$(1 - C_Y - I_Y)(Md_i) + (C_i + I_i)(Md_Y) < 0. \tag{6.86}$$

Given $(C_i + I_i) > 0$, we may rearrange equation 6.86 to generate

$$\frac{(1 - C_Y - I_Y)}{(C_i + I_i)} > -\frac{Md_Y}{Md_i} > 0. \tag{6.87}$$

That is, the condition for IS-LM stability is that the slope of the IS curve must exceed that of the LM curve:

$$\text{slope IS} > \text{slope LM} > 0. \tag{6.88}$$

Clearly, this is the opposite condition of that formally derived in chapter 4. Obviously, this change in the stability condition is exclusively the result of our new behavioral condition that $(C_i + I_i) > 0$.

Thus, the assumptions that $C_i > 0$ and $I_i > 0$ imply that in order to generate IS-LM stability the IS curve is positively sloped and steeper than the

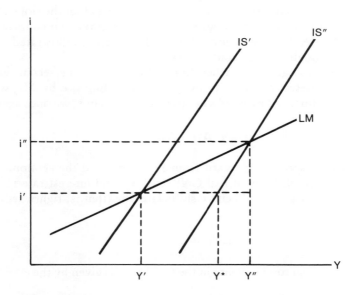

Figure 6–9. Negative Transactions Crowding Out

LM curve. A stable IS-LM equilibrium corresponding to condition 6.87 is shown in figure 6–9, at the intersection of curves IS′ and LM.

We may now briefly consider an open economy such as:

$$Y = C + I + G + X - R. \tag{6.89}$$

The additions to the aforementioned closed system are described by

$$X = \bar{X} \tag{6.90}$$

$$R = R(Y), \tag{6.91}$$

where

$$1 > \frac{dR}{dY} > 0. \tag{6.92}$$

In this system, IS-LM stability requires that

$$\frac{1 - C_Y - I_Y + R_Y}{C_i + I_i} > -\frac{Md_Y}{Md_i} > 0. \tag{6.93}$$

Thus, as in the closed system, IS-LM stability requires that the slope of the IS curve be positive and greater than that of the LM curve. To confirm condition 6.93, the reader should either follow the procedure illustrated in equations 6.80 through 6.87 or consult chapter 4.

Refer now to figure 6–9, where curves IS′ and LM intersect at real GNP level Y' and interest rate i'. Let government spending rise by ΔG, with the increase being financed by bond sales to the public. Thus, we once again have

$$\Delta G = \Delta B. \tag{6.94}$$

The IS curve is shifted rightward from IS′ to IS″, and the economy moves toward a new equilibrium at real GNP level Y'' and interest rate i''.

Observe now that the IS curve shifts laterally (that is, rightward) by the distance

$$\Delta Y_1 = Y^* - Y'. \tag{6.95}$$

However, the final total increase in the GNP level is given by the even greater distance

$$\Delta Y_2 = Y'' - Y'. \tag{6.96}$$

In terms of the GNP level, a negative transactions crowding out occurs; this negative crowding out effect is described by the magnitude

$$\Delta Y_2 - \Delta Y_1 = Y^* - Y'' < 0. \tag{6.97}$$

Moreover, a similar set of results could also have been derived in the case of our open economy.

The reason underlying this negative crowding out effect is really quite simple. In particular, as the interest rate is pushed upward as a consequence of the expansionary fiscal action, the levels of consumption and investment are raised. This raise enhances the effect of the government spending increase rather than offsetting it as in the case of standard transactions crowding out. As opposed to standard (simple) transactions crowding out, where higher interest rates reduced consumption and investment and thereby reduced the efficacy of the fiscal policy, the present case generates an expansion in the GNP level that is actually greater than the simple spendings multiplier (see equation 6.47).

Mathematically, this set of conclusions can be represented quite easily. In the simple, closed economy illustrated in figure 6–9, the government spending multiplier corresponding to the case of negative transactions crowding out (that is, distance $Y'' - Y'$) is given by

$$\frac{dY}{d\bar{G}} = \frac{Md_i}{(1 - C_Y - I_Y)Md_i + (C_i + I_i)Md_Y} = K^* > 0. \quad (6.98)$$

Meanwhile, the multiplier corresponding to the simple rightward shifting of the IS curve is given by

$$\frac{dY}{d\bar{G}} = \frac{1}{(1 - C_Y - I_Y)} = K^{**} > 0. \quad (6.99)$$

The multiplier shown in equation 6.99 also can be interpreted as corresponding to zero crowding out, as in the crude Keynesian system. Finally, the multiplier corresponding to standard transactions crowding out, under the condition that $(C_i + I_i) < 0$, is given by

$$\frac{dY}{d\bar{G}} = \frac{Md_i}{(1 - C_Y - I_Y)Md_i + (C_i + I_i)Md_Y} = K^{***} > 0. \quad (6.100)$$

Given that in the case of K^*, $(C_i + I_i) > 0$, whereas in the case of K^{***}, $(C_i + I_i) < 0$, it logically follows that

$$K^* > K^{**} > K^{***} > 0. \quad (6.101)$$

Thus, it follows that, in the circumstance where $(C_i + I_i) > 0$, as per Weber (1970, 1975), Yarrow (1975), and Izenson (1983), negative transactions crowding out is presumably experienced.

Summary

This chapter has surveyed and/or presented a number of theories of crowding out. The first case considered was the crude Classical case. The crude Classical case of crowding out implies a demand for money function that is completely interest inelastic. The result, in terms of an IS-LM analytical framework, is a completely vertical LM curve. The effect of a debt-financed increase in the level of government expenditures is a shift in the IS curve to the right. The equilibrium interest rate rises, but the level of income and the income velocity of circulation remain unchanged. In this case the increase in the interest rate results in a reduction in private investment spending and in private consumption spending that precisely offsets the increase in government expenditures. Crowding out is then complete.

By contrast, the crude Keynesian system was characterized by a completely vertical IS curve and a positively sloped LM curve. Within this context, zero crowding out was generated. However, as illustrated in several instances, it is entirely possible to experience crowding out without a vertical LM curve. Even in Keynes (1936, p. 120), there are passages that imply crowding out; as shown in figure 6–3, an increase in the level of government expenditures may result in crowding out by eroding confidence and resulting thus in an increase in liquidity preference and a decrease in the marginal efficiency of capital.

Transactions crowding out was illustrated in figure 6–4. It was shown that, even with a positively sloped LM curve (and with the IS curve negatively sloped), partial crowding out would occur as rising interest rates discouraged private sector spending. Transactions crowding out is perhaps the best known of the crowding out hypotheses. Indeed, transactions crowding out is discussed in most macroeconomics textbooks.

The theory of ultrarationality formulated by David and Scadding (1974) implies complete crowding out. For example, if households view the government sector as an extension of themselves, an increase in government spending displaces an equal amount of private investment expenditures since households would view private investment and public investment as alternative ways of achieving an increased flow of future consumption benefits. The end result of the fiscal action, then, is a zero net change in the real GNP level; the complete crowding out is characterized simply by a reallocation of the real GNP from the private sector to the government sector. This reallocation of GNP from the private sector to the public sector somewhat resembles the workings of the crude Classical system in figure 6–1.

As shown in figure 6–6, financial crowding out, which is most often associated with Friedman (1970, 1971), implies complete crowding out. In one case, this is because the deficit, if financed by bond sales to the public, allegedly absorbs savings that would have been funneled to firms for purposes of private investment. As a result, increased government spending in this case tends to be offset by an equally decreased private investment level.

A further possible explanation of crowding out is provided by portfolio crowding out and real net wealth effects. Here, a bond-financed increase (through sales to the public) in government expenditures results in an increase in household liquid wealth. Although this increase in liquid wealth may result in an increase in private consumption spending, it may also result in an increase in the aggregate demand for money. These wealth effects tend to shift both the LM and IS curves as demonstrated in figure 6–7. The net effect of these factors, together with interest-sensitive investment and consumption functions may lead to partial crowding out.

Klein (1972) has offered a hypothesis referred to as *portfolio substitution crowding out*. Klein argues that new government bond issues, because of their substitutability for commodities and money, shift the IS and LM curves and may thus cause *partial* crowding out. Klein (1972) also includes wealth effects in his model and ensuing analysis.

Based on the findings in Weber (1970, 1975), Izenson (1983), and Yarrow (1975), a model in which aggregate consumption spending and aggregate investment spending are both directly related to the interest rate can be constructed. Within this model, it can be shown that a negative transactions crowding out effect conceivably could occur (and without jeoparding the stability of the system). That is, with an expansionary fiscal action (such as $\Delta G > 0$), rising interest rates lead to increased (rather than decreased) consumption and investment and hence generate a net negative transactions crowding out effect (dY/dG rises as a result of $\partial I/\partial i > 0$ and $\partial C/\partial i > 0$). Of course, whether and to what degree one accepts the empirical findings that $\partial C/\partial i > 0$ and $\partial I/\partial i > 0$ is another matter entirely.

Additional Observations

In closing this chapter, it is appropriate to make a number of additional observations. To some extent, these observations may be helpful to the reader in the process of evaluation, acceptance, or rejection of any part of the theories of crowding out provided in this chapter.

To begin with, the survey provided here of theories of crowding out covers perhaps the better known parts of the literature. Nevertheless, this does not mean that other plausible, realistic, reasonable, or important theories of crowding out do not exist. The interested reader is referred, for additional insights into crowding out, to the contributions by Buiter (1977), Blinder and Solow (1973), Christ (1968), Eisner and Pieper (1984), Meyer (1975), and Steindl (1971), among others. Moreover, we also have not examined all of the major criticisms and/or extensions of the crowding out hypotheses examined here. For example, Smith (1939) and Cebula (1973) have both extended the analysis by Keynes (1936, p. 120) as outlined in figure 6–3. There also have been a number of criticisms of Friedman's hypothesis of financial crowding out. For instance, Van Cott and Santoni (1974) have challenged the basic tenets and conclusions of Friedman's analysis; moreover, these authors have done so rather convincingly.

Second, it has sometimes been argued that the degree of crowding out may be increased by the impact of debt-financed government spending increases, which push upward on interest rates and therefore on the value of the dollar in international currency markets. As interest rates in the United States are allegedly being pushed upward as a result of a deficit-financed fiscal action, foreign demand for dollars rises as foreign investors seek to exchange their currency for ours in order to make financial investments in the United States. If foreign demand for dollars rises as a result of bond-financed fiscal actions elevating rates of interest in this country, then the value of the dollar may increase. If this occurs, then U.S. exports would likely decline, and U.S. imports would likely increase.[10] These effects would tend to shift the IS curve downward and to the left. In turn, the real GNP level would tend to be reduced from what it otherwise might have been, and the crowding out may then be increased above what it might otherwise have been.

Next, the analysis of crowding out provided in this chapter has stressed a number of possible crowding out causes. In the interest of simplicity, we have not included an analysis of the potential economic impacts of a changing aggregate price level. In the simpler models, such as those omitting the real wealth effect, the effect of an expansionary, bond-financed fiscal action might be to elevate the aggregate price level (see chapter 5).[11] As a result the LM curve would tend to be shifted leftward due to a reduced real money supply. In turn, this would in most cases presumably result in a lower equilibrium real GNP level and hence in a greater degree of crowding out.[12] In models including a real wealth effect, the elevated aggregate price level would also act to reduce real wealth and hence to shift the IS curve leftward; consequently, the equilibrium real GNP level in such cases would tend to be even further reduced.[13] And, if real wealth also were included in the money demand function as Patinkin (1965) and others maintain a higher price level would tend to shift the LM curve by lowering real balances and hence real money demand.

In order to illustrate the impact of price level changes on the degree of crowding out, we now refer to figure 6–10, where we reconsider the simple case of transactions crowding out. In figure 6–10, LM*, IS*, and IS** are replicated from figure 6–4; furthermore, interest rates i^* and i^{**} and real GNP levels Y^*, Y^{**}, and Y' from figure 6–4 have also been replicated. Transactions crowding out, before allowing for changes in the aggregate price level, is given by

$$Y' - Y^{**}. \tag{6.102}$$

However, as a result of the aggregate price level increase resulting from the bond-financed, expansionary fiscal action, the LM curve shifts leftward (as shown in chapters 3 and 5), say from LM* to LM**. Transactions crowding out now rises to the amount

$$Y' - Y''. \tag{6.103}$$

Thus, while transactions crowding out is still only partial, the degree of crowding out is now greater than was the case before the aggregate price level increased, since

$$(Y' - Y'') > (Y' - Y^{**}). \tag{6.104}$$

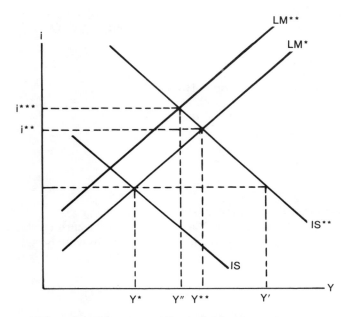

Figure 6–10. Effect of Price Increase

Clearly, as the price level rose and shifted the LM curve upward, still higher interest rates were generated. These higher interest rates in turn further diminished private sector spending and thus increased the degree of crowding out, in this case by the amount

$$(Y' - Y'') - (Y' - Y^{**}) = Y^{**} - Y'' > 0. \qquad (6.105)$$

The positive sign shown in equation 6.105 indicates an increased degree of crowding out resulting from the effect of the aggregate price level increase on the real money supply.

Finally, there is the fact that, to each reader, the plausibility or reasonableness of some crowding out theories may seem more compelling than others.[14] In turn, the reader may wish simply to combine certain aspects of one crowding out theory with selected aspects of one or more other crowding out theories.

For example, as already noted, Weber (1970, 1975) has found aggregate consumption to be an increasing function of the interest rate

$$C_i > 0. \qquad (6.106)$$

Meanwhile, the usual (conventional) assumption regarding the relationship between aggregate investment and the interest rate is given by

$$I_i < 0. \tag{6.107}$$

Combining equations 6.106 and 6.107 yields

$$(C_i + I_i) \gtreqless 0 \quad \text{as} \quad |C_i| \gtreqless |I_i|. \tag{6.108}$$

If we are given the case where

$$|C_i| = |I_i|, \tag{6.109}$$

then it follows that the IS curve is perfectly vertical.

Alternatively, the findings by Yarrow (1975) and Izenson (1983), among others, are that aggregate investment is (or may be) an increasing function of the interest rate

$$I_i > 0. \tag{6.110}$$

Meanwhile, the conventional assumption as to the impact of interest rates on aggregate consumption is given by

$$C_i < 0. \tag{6.111}$$

Clearly, it follows, given equations 6.110 and 6.111 that

$$(I_i + C_i) = 0 \quad \text{as} \quad |I_i| \gtreqless |C_i|. \tag{6.112}$$

From equation 6.112, it is apparent that if

$$|I_i| = |C_i|, \tag{6.113}$$

then the IS curve is perfectly vertical.

Refer now to figure 6–11, where the perfectly vertical IS curve IS′ is consistent with either equation 6.109 or equation 6.113. If government spending rises by ΔG and ΔG is financed by bond sales to the public, the IS curve shifts rightward by the full spendings multiplier (see equation 6.99) to, say, IS″. Obviously, as in the visually similar although behaviorally different crude Keynesian case, there will be zero crowding out under these circumstances:

$$\frac{dY}{d\overline{G}} = \frac{Md_i}{(1 - C_Y - I_Y)Md_i + (C_i + I_i)Md_Y} = \frac{1}{(1 - C_Y - I_y)}. \tag{6.114}$$

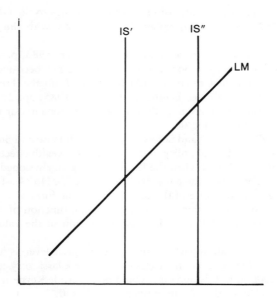

Figure 6–11. Combining Cases

This is because $C_i + I_i$ equals zero. Clearly, other possible combinations of equations 6.106 and 6.107 or 6.110 and 6.111 can be considered; furthermore, in each such case, different degrees of transactions crowding out (or of negative transactions crowding out) can be expected.

In any event, it should be stressed once again that crowding out need not be an absolute phenomenon. That is, crowding out can be either complete or partial and still be crowding out. The necessary condition, for all practical purposes, for crowding out to occur is only that dY/dG be reduced. It need not be reduced to zero, however. Moreover, dY/dG certainly need not become negative, a condition that has important implications for system stability.[15]

Notes

1. The treatment shown in figure 6–3 is similar to that in Carlson and Spencer (1975, p. 6). See also the detailed treatment in Cebula (1973).

2. The possibility that $\Delta Y > 0$ is found in Carlson and Spencer (1975, p. 6).

3. The insightful remarks by Keynes (1936, p. 119) would seem to hint at transactions crowding out.

4. Denison's Law (see Denison, 1958) concerns the observed stability in the

United States over time of the ratio of gross private savings to the GNP level. David and Scadding (1974) attempt to explain Denison's Law with the ultrarationality hypothesis.

5. See, for example, the observations by Hoelscher (1983, p. 320).

6. It is assumed that the bonds in question have not been monetized by the FED. Monetizing the deficit refers to FED purchases from the Treasury of newly issued bonds. Related to this, see Baumol and Blinder (1985, pp. 293–295).

7. See, for example, figure 6–5 illustrating ultrarationality, or figure 6–1 illustrating crude Classical crowding out.

8. Silber (1970), Blinder and Solow (1973), and Infante and Stein (1976) have found that bond-financed fiscal policy in the presence of wealth effects has an ambiguous impact on the GNP level when the IS curve is negatively sloped.

9. The reader may find the paper by Hwang and Yu (1984) of relevance here.

10. Naturally, the structure of the economy is of the form $Y = C + I + G + X - R$, where, among other things, X is a decreasing function of the value of the dollar (ceteris paribus), and R is an increasing function of the value of the dollar (ceteris paribus).

11. Of course, such an impact (on the aggregate price level) is not always to be expected. Consider, for example, the case of the crude Classical system.

12. One exception to this outcome would be the crude Keynesian system, characterized by a perfectly vertical IS curve since $C_i = I_i = 0$.

13. In open economies, a rise in the domestic price level would, ceteris paribus, tend to lower exports and raise imports, thereby shifting the IS curve leftward and implying an increased degree of crowding out if the price level increase resulted from an expansionary fiscal action.

14. Of course, the reader may feel that none of the crowding out hypotheses is appealing or valid.

15. Related to the issues of stability, crowding out, and negative multipliers, see Blinder and Solow (1973). In a different context, see also Cebula (1976), Cebula, Carlos, and Koch (1981), Hwang and Yu (1984), and Wang (1980).

References

Abrams, B.A., and M.D. Schmitz, 1978. The "Crowding Out" Effect of Government Transfers on Private Charitable Contributions, *Public Choice,* vol. 33, pp. 29–39.

Anderson, C.L., and J.L. Jordan, 1968. Monetary and Fiscal Actions: A Test of Their Relative Importance in Economic Stabilization, *Federal Reserve Bank of St. Louis Review,* November, pp. 11–24.

Arestis, P., 1979. The "Crowding Out" of Private Expenditures by Fiscal Actions: An Empirical Investigation, *Public Finance/Finances Publiques,* vol. 34, pp. 19–41.

Baumol, W.J., and A.S. Blinder, 1985. *Economics.* New York: Harcourt, Brace, and Jovanovich.

Blinder, A.S., and R.M. Solow, 1973. Does Fiscal Policy Matter? *Journal of Public Economics,* vol. 2, pp. 318–337.

Buiter, W.H., 1977. Crowding Out and the Effectiveness of Fiscal Policy, *Journal of Public Economics,* vol. 7, pp. 309–328.

Carlson, K.M., and R.W. Spencer, 1975. Crowding Out and Its Critics, *Federal Reserve Bank of St. Louis Review,* December, pp. 1–19.

Cebula, R.J., 1973. Deficit Spending, Expectations, and Fiscal Policy Effectiveness, *Public Finance/Finances Publiques,* vol. 28, pp. 362–370.

Cebula, R.J., 1976. A Brief Note on Economic Policy Effectiveness, *Southern Economic Journal,* vol. 43, pp. 1174–1176.

Cebula, R.J., 1980. IS-LM Stability and Economic Policy Effectiveness: Further Observations, *Journal of Macroeconomics,* vol. 2, pp. 181–184.

Cebula, R.J., C. Carlos, and J.M. Koch, 1981. The "Crowding Out" Effect of Federal Government Outlay Decisions: An Empirical Note, *Public Choice,* vol. 36, pp. 329–336.

Christ, C.F., 1968. A Simple Macroeconomic Model with a Government Budget Restraint, *Journal of Political Economy,* vol. 76, pp. 53–67.

David, P.A., and J.L. Scadding, 1974. Private Savings: Ultrarationality, Aggregation, and Denison's Law, *Journal of Political Economy,* vol. 82, pp. 225–249.

Denison, E.F., 1958. A Note on Private Saving, *Review of Economics and Statistics,* vol. 40, pp. 261–267.

Dwyer, G.F., 1982. Inflation and Government Deficits, *Economic Inquiry,* vol. 20, pp. 315–329.

Eisner, R., and P.J. Pieper, 1984. A New View of the Federal Debt and Budget Deficit, *American Economic Review,* vol. 74, pp. 11–29.

Evans, P., 1985. Do Large Deficits Produce High Interest Rates? *American Economic Review,* vol. 75, pp. 68–87.

Friedman, M., 1970. A Theoretical Framework for Monetary Analysis, *Journal of Political Economy,* vol. 78, pp. 193–238.

Friedman, M., 1971. A Monetary Theory of Nominal Income, *Journal of Political Economy,* vol. 79, pp. 323–337.

Hoelscher, G.P., 1983. Federal Borrowing and Short-Term Interest Rates, *Southern Economic Journal,* vol. 50, pp. 319–333.

Hwang, B.K., and E.S. Yu, 1984. Wealth Effects, IS-LM Stability and the Efficacy of Economic Policies, *Journal of Macroeconomics,* vol. 6, pp. 229–234.

Infante, E.F., and J.L. Stein, 1976. Does Fiscal Policy Matter? *Journal of Monetary Economics,* vol. 2, pp. 473–500.

Izenson, M.S., 1983. A Brief Note on the Relationship Between Investment and the Interest Rate in the United States, *Economic Notes,* vol. 12, pp. 135–138.

Keran, M.W., 1969. Monetary and Fiscal Influences on Economic Activity—The Historical Evidence, *Federal Reserve Bank of St. Louis Review,* November, pp. 5–24.

Keran, M.W., 1970. Monetary and Fiscal Influences on Economic Activity: The Foreign Experience, *Federal Reserve Bank of St. Louis Review,* February, pp. 16–28.

Keynes, J.M., 1936. *The General Theory of Employment, Interest, and Money.* New York: Harcourt, Brace and Company.

Klein, J.J., 1972. More on the Analysis of Fiscal Policy and Bond Financing, *Economic Notes,* vol. 1, pp. 50–60.

Meyer, L.H., 1975. The Balance Sheet of Identity, the Government Financing Constraint, and the Crowding Out Effect, *Journal of Monetary Economics,* vol. 4, pp. 65–78.

Meyer, P.A., 1983. Money Multipliers and the Slopes of IS-LM, *Southern Economic Journal,* vol. 49, pp. 226–229.

Musgrave, R., 1959. *The Theory of Public Finance.* New York: McGraw-Hill.

Patinkin, D., 1948. Price Flexibility and Full Employment, *American Economic Review,* vol. 38, pp. 543–564.

Patinkin, D., 1965. *Money, Interest, and Prices,* 2nd ed. New York: Harper and Row.

Silber, W.L., 1970. Fiscal Policy in IS-LM Analysis: A Correction, *Journal of Money, Credit and Banking,* vol. 2, pp. 461–473.

Smith, D.T., 1939. Is Deficit Spending Practical? *Harvard Business Review,* vol. 45, pp. 36–42.

Steindl, F.G., 1971. A Simple Macroeconomic Model with a Government Budget Restraint: A Comment, *Journal of Political Economy,* vol. 79, pp. 675–679.

Sullivan, B.P., 1976. Crowding Out Estimated from Large-Scale Econometric Model, *Federal Reserve Bank of Dallas, Business Review,* June, pp. 1–7.

Van Cott, T.N., and G. Santoni, 1974. Friedman Versus Tobin: A Comment, *Journal of Political Economy,* vol. 82, pp. 883–885.

Wang, L.F.S., 1980. IS-LM Stability and Economic Policy Effectiveness: A Note, Journal of Macroeconomics, vol. 2, pp. 175–179.

Weber, W.E., 1970. The Effect of Interest Rates on Aggregate Consumption, *American Economic Review,* vol. 60, pp. 591–600.

Weber, W.E., 1975. Interest Rates, Inflation, and Consumer Expenditures, *American Economic Review,* vol. 65, pp. 843–858.

Whitmore, H.W., 1980. Unbalanced Government Budgets, Private Asset Holdings, and the Traditional Comparative Statics Multipliers, *Journal of Macroeconomics,* vol. 2, pp. 129–157.

Yarrow, G.K., 1975. Growth Maximization and the Firm's Investment Function, *Southern Economic Journal,* vol. 41, pp. 580–592.

Zahn, F., 1978. A Flow of Funds Analysis of Crowding Out, *Southern Economic Journal,* vol. 45, pp. 195–206.

7
Crowding Out: Search for a
Transmission Mechanism

As shown in chapter 6, crowding out can in theory assume a large variety of different forms including Classical crowding out, simple transactions crowding out, ultrarationality, financial crowding out, portfolio crowding out, and portfolio substitution crowding out. Of these forms, transaction crowding out is probably the best known. Figure 7–1 illustrates the transactions crowding out impact of a rise in government spending financed entirely by Treasury bond sales to the private sector of the economy. The IS curve shifts upward from IS* to IS**, and the economy moves from its original IS-LM equilibrium at Y^*, i^* to a new IS-LM equilibrium at Y^{**}, i^{**}. Transactions crowding out is indicated by the distance from Y^{**} to Y'. Note that a key trait of this form of crowding out is a net rise in the rate of interest. Other forms of crowding out including portfolio crowding out and portfolio substitution crowding out are also characterized by rising interest rate levels.

Numerous empirical studies investigating the possible existence of crowding out and the degree of crowding out have appeared (see, for example, Abrams and Schmitz, 1978; Anderson and Jordan, 1968; Arestis, 1979; Cebula, Carlos, and Koch, 1981; Keran, 1969, 1970; Sullivan, 1976; and Zahn, 1978. Although these studies attempt to measure the degree of crowding out, they do not attempt to identify or verify the existence of the actual mechanism by which crowding out may be transmitted to the economy at large. For instance, the studies cited above do not attempt to verify whether a federal budget deficit exercises any impact on interest rates as would be the case for transactions crowding out, portfolio crowding out, and portfolio substitution crowding out. As indicated in the following section of this chapter, however, recent literature has appeared that attempts to address this issue.

Literature on Federal Borrowing and Interest Rates

A number of recent studies have focused on the possible impact of federal government borrowings on short-term interest rates. For instance, Hoelscher

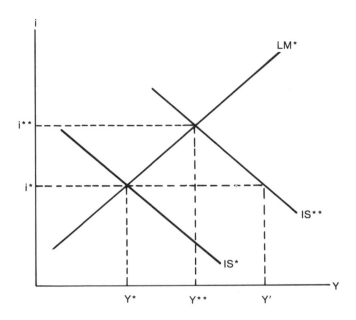

Figure 7–1. Simple Transactions Crowding Out Case

(1983, p. 319) empirically examines "the effects of federal government borrowing on short-term interest rates." Hoelscher's analysis is based on regressions that test whether the level of federal borrowing is a statistically significant determinant of the three-month Treasury bill rate. Hoelscher (1983, p. 319) obtains extremely low t values on the relevant coefficients and hence concludes that "Federal borrowing is a relatively unimportant . . . determinant of short-term rates." Accordingly, Hoelscher (p. 332) concludes that "to the extent that private expenditures are sensitive only to short-term rates, then Federal borrowing does not have financial crowding out effects." Hoelscher (1983) comes to this conclusion despite his confusion over the distinction between transactions crowding out and financial crowding out. Makin (1983) has also examined the impact of federal government borrowing on the three-month Treasury bill rate. Like Hoelscher (1983), Makin (1983, p. 381) finds federal borrowing to have very little (if any) impact on the three-month Treasury bill rate: "Based on equation 6(b) a $100 billion deficit would elevate short-term interest rates by only 10 basis points." Accordingly, Makin (p. 382) concludes that "Overall, the results reported here regarding the possible significance of 'crowding out' can only be judged as 'mixed to weak.'"

Results very similar to those in Hoelscher (1983) and Makin (1983) have also been obtained by Motley (1983) and in the empirical analysis of the three-month Treasury bill rate by Mascaro and Meltzer (1983). Interestingly, Mascaro and Meltzer also find the interest rate yield on ten-year U.S. government bonds to be unaffected by federal budget deficits.

On the other hand, a recent comment by Barth, Iden, and Russek (1985, p. 556) on the Hoelscher (1983) paper finds that, after adjusting the federal deficit for the effects of cyclical activity, the resulting structural deficit has a "positive and highly significant impact on the three-month Treasury bill rate." A study by Evans (1985) examines the impact of federal deficits on the three-month Treasury bill rate (and selected other interest rates) for four separate time periods in the U.S. history (the Civil War period, World War I, World War II, and October 1970 to December 1983). Evans's analysis may be marred by multicolinearity problems between two of his so-called exogenous variables, namely, the ratio of real federal spending to trend real national income (GR) and the ratio of the real federal deficit to trend real national income (DR). This is because a pattern of both federal spending budget growth and federal deficit growth is characteristic of each of the four periods of Evans's investigation. Nevertheless, like the earlier studies by Hoelscher (1983), Makin (1983), Motley (1983), and Mascaro and Meltzer (1983, p. 68) finds "no evidence for a positive association between deficits and interest rates."

All of these studies are concerned ultimately with the possible crowding out that can result from federal deficits (borrowing). Moreover, in conjunction with this concern for crowding out, all of these studies stress the impact of deficits on the three-month Treasury bill rate; the only exceptions are the paper by Mascaro and Meltzer (1983), which also examines the long-term rate (ten years) on U.S. government bonds but finds the long-term rate to be unaffected by federal deficits and the paper by Evans (1985), which also considers, to some degree, selected alternative interest rate measures, each of which is insensitive to federal deficits. There is a problem with this entire procedure of stressing the three-month Treasury bill rate, however. In particular, firms make investment decisions predicated, among other factors, on long-term interest rates, not simply short-term interest rates. As Hoelscher (1983, p. 332) concedes, "If private expenditures are also sensitive to medium or long-term rates, then . . . crowding out is possible." As a result, it might have been preferable for previous studies to have stressed the potential impact of federal borrowing on long-term rates (such as the average interest rate yield on longer-term Treasury bonds).

The present chapter seeks to ascertain the impact of federal borrowing on long-term interest rates. We begin with a simple loanable funds model and generate a reduced form equation for the determination of the interest rate. Next we develop an empirical analysis of the impact of federal borrowing on the interest rate yield on long-term U.S. government bonds.

A Simple Loanable Funds Model

In order to help provide insights into the interest rate impact of federal government borrowing, a simple loanable funds model is developed. Actually, the IS-LM paradigm is the most common frame of reference for the study of the potential interest rate effects of federal borrowing or federal deficits (see, for example, Evans, 1985 and Mascaro and Meltzer 1983). In this chapter we use a loanable funds model simply to illustrate an alternative perspective on the issue. Technically, the highlighted explanatory variables could be shown to be derivable from either framework. As Patinkin (1965) and others have stressed so often, Walras's Law dictates that in a three-market economy consisting of commodities, money, and bonds, IS-LM equilibrium implies bond market equilibrium. In turn, bond market equilibrium requires that the private sector's excess demand for bonds be precisely equal to the public sector's excess supply of bonds. This condition may be stated in simple form as

$$DB - SB = F, \tag{7.1}$$

where DB is the real private sector demand for bonds, SB is the real private sector supply of bonds, and F represents real net borrowing by the Federal government from the private sector.

Based on arguments in Patinkin (1965, chapter 10), Hoelscher (1983, p. 321), and other studies, it can be reasonably argued that

$$DB = f(r, \dot{P}^e, \dot{Y}, \ldots) \tag{7.2}$$

$$SB = g(r, \dot{P}^e, \dot{Y}\ldots), \tag{7.3}$$

where r is the nominal rate of interest, $\dot{P}^e$ is the expected rate of inflation, and $\dot{Y}$ is the rate of growth of real GNP. The assumed signs on the partial derivations are given by

$$\frac{\partial f}{\partial r} > 0, \frac{\partial f}{\partial \dot{P}^e} < 0, \frac{\partial f}{\partial \dot{Y}} > 0 \tag{7.4}$$

$$\frac{\partial g}{\partial r} < 0, \frac{\partial g}{\partial \dot{P}^e} > 0, \frac{\partial g}{\partial \dot{Y}} > 0 \tag{7.5}$$

Equations 7.4 and 7.5 indicate that, in accord with the conventional wisdom, private sector bond demand is an increasing function of the interest rate, whereas private sector bond supply is a decreasing function of the interest rate. These commonplace arguments are found in Patinkin (1965) and Hoelscher (1983), as well as elsewhere. In equations 7.4 and 7.5, we also see that private sector bond demand is a decreasing function of the expected inflation rate. This is because a greater inflation rate would reduce the real value of bond holdings to would-be or actual bond holders. On the other hand, the private sector bond supply is an increasing function of the expected inflation rate since, ceteris paribus, a higher inflation rate would enable the bond issuer to ultimately repay the borrowed funds in cheaper and cheaper dollars. These arguments are compatible with Hoelscher (1983, p. 321). Finally, private sector bond demand and supply are presumably both increasing functions of the growth rate of real GNP. As Patinkin (1965, p. 215) argues, the more rapidly real GNP rises, the more rapidly disposable real income increases, and thus the more rapidly real saving and real private sector bond demand increase. Moreover, the more rapidly real GNP rises, the more rapidly the real supply of bonds rises as the business sector accelerates its credit demands for, as Patinkin notes (pp. 216–217), purchases of "plant, equipment, and inventories."

If equations 7.2 and 7.3 are both substituted into equation 7.1, a reduction form equation with the interest rate expressed as the dependent variable may be generated. Such an equation is given by

$$r = h(F, \dot{P}^e, \dot{Y}). \tag{7.6}$$

On the basis of equations 7.4 and 7.5, it follows that we should expect

$$\frac{\partial h}{\partial F} > 0, \frac{\partial h}{\partial \dot{P}^e} > 0, \frac{\partial h}{\partial \dot{Y}} \gtrless 0. \tag{7.7}$$

The validity of these arguments, as well as others, will be examined empirically in the following section of this chapter.

Empirical Analysis

On the basis of the simple model in the preceding section, we begin our empirical analysis with the following three regression equations:

$$r_{LT} = a_{0t} + a_1 F_t / Y_t + \mu_1 \tag{7.8}$$

$$r_{LT} = b_{0t} + b_1 F_t / Y_t + b_2 [(\dot{P}_t + \dot{P}_{t-4})/2)] + \mu_2 \tag{7.9}$$

$$r_{LT} = c_{0t} + c_1 F_t / Y_t + c_2 [(\dot{P}_t + \dot{P}_{t-4})/2)] + c_3 \dot{Y}_t + \mu_2 . \tag{7.10}$$

where r_{LT} equals interest rate yield on ten-year U.S. government bonds in quarter t; a_{0t}, b_{0t}, c_{0t} equals constant terms; F_t equals real value of sales of ten-year U.S. government bonds in quarter t, expressed in annualized terms; Y_t equals real GNP in quarter t, expressed in annualized terms; $\dot{P}_t$ equals actual inflation rate of the CPI, during quarter t; $\dot{P}_{t-4}$ equals actual inflation rate of the CPI, lagged four quarters; $\dot{Y}_t$ equals the percentage rate of growth of real GNP; and μ_1, $\mu_2\mu_3$ equals stochastic error terms. The data to be examined are all quarterly. The time period runs from 1973:1 through 1985:2.

The variable F_t includes all federal government borrowings in the form of ten-year U.S. government bonds transacted in quarter t.[1] It includes both refinancing and deficits in the form of ten-year U.S. government bonds. The existing literature has generally focused on the aggregate federal budget deficit and its impact on the ninety-day Treasury bill rate. This focus is both too broad and too narrow. It is too broad insofar as it includes bonds other then ninety-day Treasury bills; it is too narrow since it omits borrowing for purposes of refinancing. In its formulation of the variable F_t, this chapter has attempted to avoid these two shortcomings. Moreover, following Evans (1985) and Hoelscher (1983, p. 324), the variable F_t is scaled (divided) by variable Y_t in order to allow for the secular drift of real GNP over time. From another viewpoint, we divide F_t by Y_t because federal government borrowings should be evaluated in relation to the size of the economy that must finance them.

Next we come to the issue of expected inflation. There are a number of ways in which to specify this component of the model. One way to measure expected inflation is to use a distributed lag on past rates of inflation, as in Feldstein and Eckstein (1970), Yohe and Karnosky (1969), and other studies. Another way is to resort to survey data such as presented in Carlson (1977); this procedure was followed, for example, by Hoelscher (1983). Another possibility is the rational expectations approach followed, for example, by Mascaro and Meltzer (1983). Naturally, based on the notion developed in Gibson (1970, p. 34) that "expected price changes do appear to be related to past changes," one can develop an enormous variety of possible other specifications.

We have dealt with two forms of an inflation expectations function, one being a distributed lag formulation of the variety adopted by Feldstein and Eckstein (1970) and the other being simply the unweighted average of current actual inflation ($\dot{P}_t$) and the rate of actual inflation lagged four quarters ($\dot{P}_{t-4}$). In examining a large number of estimations, it was found that the simpler formulation of ($\dot{P}_t + \dot{P}_{t-4})/2$ actually provided the better explanatory power, and without materially altering other results in the estimations. Hence, we adopt this simpler form. Of course, for the numerous estimations in which inflationary expectations were not addressed, the choice between these two alternatives is literally of no consequence.

The ordinary least squares (OLS) estimates of equations 7.8, 7.9, and 7.10 are given by equations 7.11, 7.12, and 7.13, respectively:

$$r_{LT} = 7.31 + \underset{(+8.99)}{44.501} \ F_t/Y_t, \ DF = 48, R^2 = 0.63, R^2 = 0.62, \quad (7.11)$$

$$DW = 1.35$$

$$r_{LT} = 5.52 + \underset{(+10.11)}{43.421} \ F_t/Y_t + \underset{(+4.12)}{2.81} \ [(\dot{P}_t = \dot{P}_{t-4})/2] \quad (7.12)$$

$$DF = 47, \quad R^2 = 0.73, \quad R^2 = 0.72, \quad DW = 1.46$$

$$r_{LT} = +5.45 + \underset{(+9.72)}{42.096} \ F_t/Y_t + \underset{(+4.08)}{2.80} \ [(\dot{P}_t = \dot{P}_{t-4})/2 \quad (7.13)$$

$$+ \underset{(+0.35)}{0.01} \ \dot{Y}_t,$$

$$DF = 46, \quad R^2 = 0.73, \quad R^2 = 0.72, \quad DW = 1.46$$

where terms in parentheses beneath coefficients are *t*-values.

In all of these equations, the coefficients on the federal borrowings variable ($= F_t/Y_t$) and the simple inflation expectations variable [$\dot{P}_t + \dot{P}_{t-4})/2$]) are positive and statistically significant at far beyond the 0.01 level.[2] The coefficient on the variable $\dot{Y}_t$ is positive but not significant at an acceptable level. Thus, the findings shown in equations 7.11 through 7.13 are consistent with the predictions in equation 7.7. Moreover, and most important, the results in equations 7.11, 7.12, and 7.13 indicate that long-term federal government borrowings in the form of ten-year bonds seem to exercise a positive and significant impact on the interest rate yield on those bonds.

Of course, in the analysis of the interest rate impact of federal government borrowings, it may be appropriate to allow for factors besides F_t/Y_t, [$(\dot{P}_t + \dot{P}_{t-4})/2$], and $\dot{Y}_t$. For instance, Mascaro and Meltzer (1983), Makin (1983), Motley (1983), and Evans (1985) all somehow allow for the impact of monetary growth ($+$, $-$, or 0). Consider, for example, the following four regressions:

$$r_{LT} = d_{0t} + d_1 F_t/Y_t + d_2[(\dot{P}_t + \dot{P}_{t-4})/2] + d_3 \dot{Y}_t \quad (7.14)$$

$$+ d_4(Ml_t/Y_t) + \mu_4$$

$$r_{LT} = e_{0t} + e_1 F_t/Y_t + e_2[(\dot{P}_t + \dot{P}_{t-4})/2] + e_3 \dot{Y}_t \quad (7.15)$$

$$+ e_4(M1_{t-4}/Y_{t-4}) + \mu_5$$

$$r_{Lt} = \bar{d}_{0t} + \bar{d}_1 F_t/Y_t + \bar{d}_2 M1_t/Y_t + \bar{d}_3 \dot{Y}_t + \bar{\mu}_4 \qquad (7.16)$$

$$r_{LT} = \bar{e}_{0t} + \bar{e}_{1t} F_t/Y_t + \bar{e}_2 M1_{t-4}/Y_{t-4} + \bar{e}_3 \dot{Y}_t + \bar{\mu}_5, \qquad (7.17)$$

where d_{0t}, e_{0t}, $\bar{d}_{0t}$, $\bar{e}_{0t}$ equals constant terms; $M1_t$ equals real value of the seasonally adjusted total $M1$ measure of the money stock in quarter t; and μ_4, μ_5, $\bar{\mu}_4$, $\bar{d}_5$ equals stochastic terms. Clearly, the monetary variable $M1_t/Y_t$ in equations 7.14 and 7.16 is unlagged, whereas the monetary variable in equations 7.15 and 7.17 allows a four-quarter outside lag in the effects of monetary changes. In any event, the conventional wisdom tells us that the expected sign on coefficients d_4 or e_4, or $\bar{d}_4$ or $\bar{e}_4$ is negative.

As it turns out, including both an inflation expectations variable, such as $[(\dot{P}_t + \dot{P}_{t-4})/2]$, and a monetary variable such as $M1_t/Y_t$ or $M1_{t-4}/Y_{t-4}$, in the same equation does not pose any significant multicolinearity problems. In point of fact, the zero-order correlation coefficients between $[(\dot{P}_t = \dot{P}_{t-4}/2]$ on the one hand and $M1_t/Y_t$ or $M1_{t-4}/Y_{t-4}$ on the other hand are -0.396 and -0.472, respectively. This is apparently due to the fact that the inflation variable is a rate of change, that is, a dynamic variable, whereas $M1_t/Y_t$ and $M1_{t-4}/Y_{t-4}$ are not rates of change, that is, they are not dynamic variables.

The OLS estimations of equations 7.14 through 7.17 are given by equations 7.18 through 7.21, respectively:[3]

$$r_{Lt} = 16.851 + \underset{(+2.46)}{20.044} \ F_t/Y_t + \underset{(1.88)}{1.63} \ [(\dot{P}_t + \dot{P}_{t-4})/2] \qquad (7.18)$$

$$- \underset{(-0.29)}{0.01} \ \dot{Y}_t - \underset{(-2.98)}{38.04} \ (M1_t/Y_t),$$

$$DF = 45, \quad R^2 = 0.77, \quad \bar{R}^2 = 0.75, \quad DW = 1.30,$$

$$r_{Lt} = 12.963 + \underset{(+4.07)}{30.362} \ F_t/Y_t + \underset{(+2.04)}{1.57} \ [(\dot{P}_t + \dot{P}_{t-4})/2] \qquad (7.19)$$

$$- \underset{(-0.26)}{0.01} \ \dot{Y}_t - \underset{(-2.09)}{34.48} \ (M1_{t-4}/Y_{t-4}),$$

$$DF = 45, \quad R^2 = 0.75, \quad \bar{R}^2 = 0.73, \quad DW = 1.31,$$

$$r_{Lt} = 17.502 + \underset{(-3.87)}{23.942} \ F_t/Y_t + \underset{(-4.65)}{51.96} \ M1_t/Y_t \qquad (7.20)$$

$$- \underset{(-0.88)}{0.034} \ Y_t,$$

$$DF = 46, \quad R^2 = 0.75, \quad \bar{R}^2 = 0.74, \quad DW = 1.29$$

$$r_{Lt} = 15.908 + \underset{(+4.19)}{25.116} \; F_t/Y_t - \underset{(-4.31)}{41.90} \; M1_{t-4}/Y_{t-4} \qquad (7.21)$$

$$- \underset{(-0.86)}{0.02} \; \dot{Y}_t,$$

$$DF = 46, \quad R^2 = 0.74, \quad \bar{R} = 0.73, \quad DW = 1.28.$$

In addition, in the interest of providing further potential insights, we also substitute variable $\dot{Y}_{t-4}$ for variable $\dot{Y}_t$ in equation 7.16. The OLS results for equation 7.16, thus modified, are given by equation 7.22:

$$r_{Lt} = 20.922 + \underset{(+2.12)}{13.858} \; F_t/Y_t - \underset{(-5.13)}{67.59} \; M1_t/Y_t \qquad (7.22)$$

$$- \underset{(-0.64)}{0.02} \; \dot{Y}_{t-4},$$

$$DF = 46, \quad R^2 = 0.76, \quad \bar{R} = 0.75, \quad DW = 1.09.$$

In view of the continued insignificance of the coefficient on variable $\dot{Y}_t$, (as well as $\dot{Y}_{t-4}$), not only in estimation 7.13 but also in estimations 7.18 through 7.22, we also estimate equations 7.14 and 7.15 without the variable $\dot{Y}_t$. The results are given below in equations 7.23 and 7.24, respectively:

$$r_{Lt} = 16.481 + \underset{(+2.54)}{20.909} \; F_t/Y_t - \underset{(+1.99)}{1.28} \; [(\dot{P}_t + \dot{P}_{t-4})/2] \qquad (7.23)$$

$$- \underset{(-3.11)}{37.83} \; (M_t/Y_t),$$

$$DF = 46, \quad R^2 = 0.77, \quad \bar{R} = 0.76, \quad DW = 1.28,$$

$$r_{Lt} = 12.648 + \underset{(+4.18)}{30.595} \; F_t/Y_t - \underset{(+2.08)}{1.62} \; [(\dot{P}_t + \dot{P}_{t-4})/2] \qquad (7.24)$$

$$- \underset{(-2.12)}{33.25} \; (M_{t-4}/Y_{t-4}),$$

$$DF = 46, \quad R^2 = 0.75, \quad \bar{R} = 0.74, \quad DW = 1.30.$$

Estimations 7.18 through 7.24 all reveal a persistent pattern. To begin with, our simple surrogate for anticipated inflation always exhibits a positive and reasonably significant (roughly, at the 0.05 level) impact on the r_{Lt} variable. The monetary variable, whether unlagged $M1_t/Y_t$ or lagged four quarters $M1_{t-4}/Y_{t-4}$), always has a negative and significant impact on the r_{Lt} variable. Finally, and from the viewpoint of this chapter, most important, the coefficients on the federal borrowings variable (F_t/Y_t) are consistently positive and significant at beyond the 0.01 level. It should be observed that in equivalent estimations (to equations 7.18, 7.19, 7.23, and 7.24) where a distributed lag form of inflation expectations function of the form used in Feldstein and Eckstein (1970) was adopted [in lieu of $(\dot{P}_t + \dot{P}_{t-4}(/2]$, the basic results were very similar to those shown in equations 7.18, 7.19, 7.23, and 7.24. In addition, it should be noted that dropping either the expected inflation variable or the monetary variable from any of the equations shown in here or from any of the several dozen additional equations estimated but not shown here still leaves the coefficient on variable F_t/Y_t both positive and highly significant.

While the results so far seem to clarify the impact of sales (in real terms) of ten-year U.S. government bonds on the interest rate yield on ten-year U.S. government bonds, it may be appropriate to delve a bit further into the issue at hand. For example, it is reasonable to argue that ninety-day Treasury bills are, in the eyes of investors, significant substitutes for ten-year government bonds. Indeed, we take the position that these alternative bond issues, while not perfect substitutes, are nevertheless highly substitutable for one another. Accordingly, higher rates on ninety-day Treasury bills would theoretically tend to mandate at least somewhat higher rates on ten-year government bonds, ceteris paribus. To examine this possibility we estimate the following four equations:

$$r_{Lt} = f_{0t} + f_t F_t / Y_t + f_2 [(\dot{P}_t + \dot{P}_{t-4}(/2] \qquad (7.25)$$
$$+ f_3 (M 1_t / Y_t) + f_4 TR_t + \mu_6$$

$$r_{Lt} = g_{0t} + g_1 F_t / Y_t + g_2 [(\dot{P}_t + \dot{P}_{t-4})/2 \qquad (7.26)$$
$$+ g_3 (M 1_{t-4} / Y_{t-4}) + g_4 TR_t + \mu_7$$

$$r_{Lt} = h_{0t} + h_1 F_t / Y_t + h_2 [(\dot{P}_t + \dot{P}_{t-4})/2] + h_3 TR_t + \mu_8 \qquad (7.27)$$

$$r_{Lt} = \bar{h}_{0t} + \bar{h}_1 F_t / Y_t + \bar{h}_2 M 1_t / Y_t \qquad (7.28)$$
$$+ \bar{h}_3 TR_t + \bar{\mu}_8 ,$$

where $f_{0t}, g_{0t}, h_{0t}, \bar{h}_{0t}$ equals constant terms; TR_t equals the ninety-day Treasury bill rate, quarter t; and $\mu_6, \mu_7, \mu_8, \bar{\mu}_8$ equals stochastic error terms. If, as argued, ninety-day Treasury bills are, in the eyes of investors, substitutes for ten-year U.S. government bonds, then we would expect coefficients f_4, g_4, h_3, and $\bar{h}_3$ to be positive.

The OLS estimates of equations 7.25, 7.26, 7.27, and 7.28 are given by equations 7.29, 7.30, 7.31, and 7.32, respectively:

$$r_{Lt} = 4.697 + \underset{(+4.47)}{24.580\, F_t/Y_t} + \underset{(+1.47)}{0.64\ [(\dot{P}_t + \dot{P}_{t-4})/2]} \tag{7.29}$$

$$- \underset{(-0.25)}{3.02(M1_t/Y_t)} + \underset{(+6.96)}{0.45\, TR_t,}$$

$$DF = 45, \quad R^2 = 0.90, \quad \bar{R}^2 = 0.89, \quad DW = 1.49,$$

$$r_{Lt} = 4.029 + \underset{(+5.01)}{28.511\, F_t/Y_t} + \underset{(+1.50)}{0.76\ [(\dot{P}_t + \dot{P}_{t-4})/2]} \tag{7.30}$$

$$- \underset{(-0.29)}{2.69(M1_{t-4}/Y_{t-4})} + \underset{(+6.08)}{0.44\, TR_t,}$$

$$DF = 45, \quad R^2 = 0.89, \quad \bar{R}^2 = 0.88, \quad DW = 1.55,$$

$$r_{Lt} = 4.021 + \underset{(+7.54)}{25.642\, F_t/Y_t} + \underset{(+1.71)}{0.68\ [(\dot{P}_t + \dot{P}_{t-4})/2]} \tag{7.31}$$

$$+ \underset{(+8.14)}{0.46\, TR_t,}$$

$$DF = 46, \quad R^2 = 0.90, \quad \bar{R}^2 = 0.89, \quad DW = 1.60,$$

$$r_{Lt} = 4.095 + \underset{(+7.09)}{26.914\, F_t/Y_t} - \underset{(-3.60)}{4.35\ M1_t/Y_t} + \underset{(+7.01)}{0.48\ TR_t,}$$

$$DF = 46, \quad R^2 = 0.91, \quad \bar{R} = 0.90, \quad DW = 1.61, \tag{7.32}$$

The coefficient on the ninety-day Treasury bill rate is positive and highly significant in all four estimations. In addition, the variable TR_t adds measurably to the explanatory power of the model. Moreover, we once again find that long-term real federal government borrowings (relative to real GNP) in the form of ten-year bonds seem to exercise a positive and significant impact on the interest rate yield on those bonds. The same basic outcome also is generated if we substitute variable $M1_{t-4}/Y_{t-4}$ for variable $M1_t/Y_t$ in equations 7.28 and 7.32.

Of course, it is reasonable to expect that there may exist a bidirectional relationship between r_{Lt} and TR_t. To examine this possibility a variety of two-equation systems were estimated by two-stage least squares (2SLS). In all cases, r_{Lt} and TR_t were found to in fact exercise a signficant positive impact on one another. Perhaps more importantly, however, it was found in all cases that the coefficient on variable F_t/Y_t was positive and highly significant (at beyond the 0.01 level) in the equation explaining variable r_{Lt}.

Naturally, there are other model specifications that might reasonably be considered. For example, in order to allow for partial adjustment of the interest rate to changes in the explanatory variables, it may be appropriate to include a one-quarter lag of the interest rate series as a right-hand side variable. To examine such a specification, consider the following equation:

$$r_{Lt} = i_{0t} + i_1 F_t / Y_t + i_2 [(\dot{P}_t + \dot{P}_{t-4})/2] + i_3 r_{Lt-1} + \mu_9 \tag{7.33}$$

where i_{0t} is a constant term and, μ_9 is a stochastic error term.

The OLS estimate of equation 7.33 is given by:

$$r_{Lt} = 1.017 + \underset{(+7.78)}{26.101} F_t / Y_t + \underset{(+2.19)}{0.69} [(\dot{P}_t + \dot{P}_{t-4})/2] \tag{7.34}$$

$$+ \underset{(+8.17)}{0.65} r_{Lt-1},$$

$$R^2 = 0.93, \quad \bar{R}^2 = 0.91, \quad DW = 1.42.$$

The model, inclusive of the variable r_{Lt-1}, now explains over 90 percent of the variation in the dependent variable. The coefficient on the lagged interest rate variable is positive and is significant at far beyond the 0.01 level. This finding is, in principle, consistent with the empirical findings in the earlier studies by Barth, Iden, and Russek (1985) and Hoelscher (1983). The coefficient on the inflationary expectations variable is significant at roughly the 0.05 level; this result is consistent with the most of the other findings in this chapter. Finally, we once again observe a positive and highly significant coefficient on the F_t / Y_t variable.

Other regressions including r_{Lt-1} as a right-hand side variable have also been estimated. These estimations have included a variety of additional independent variables. For nearly all cases, the coefficient on variable r_{Lt-1} remained positive and significant. Furthermore, in all cases, the coefficient on variable F_t / Y_t was positive and highly significant.

In closing this section, it should be noted that we have dealt with several economic systems in which the interest rate variable is determined (at least potentially) by federal borrowing in the form of F_t / Y_t. Of course, as a practical matter, a higher value for r_{Lt} theoretically might also imply a higher level of debt service and hence a possible need for even greater federal borrowing. Of course, if in fact the volume of total federal borrowing rises, only a portion (<1) of that borrowing will likely be in the form of ten-year bonds. Nevertheless, it would seem that a possible bi-directional relationship might exist between variables r_{Lt} and F_t / Y_t. To test this possibility, several two-equation systems were estimated by 2SLS.[4] In none of the estimations was r_{Lt} a significant determinant of F_t / Y_t. On the other hand, the federal borrowing variable (F_t / Y_t) exercised a consistently positive, statistically significant impact on the ten-year rate (r_{Lt}). Such findings reaffirm the other results presented in this chapter.

Conclusion

This chapter has empirically examined the potential impact of federal government borrowings in the form of ten-year bonds on the interest rate yield on ten-year U.S. government bonds. In all cases, the variable F_t/Y_t (as defined) exercised a positive and significant impact on the variable r_{Lt} (as defined). Moreover, numerous other specifications involving different lag structures and/or different explanatory variables were estimated.[5] In every case, F_t/Y_t had a positive and significant impact on r_{Lt}. In a small number of instances, modest multicolinearity problems were encountered. Nevertheless, despite this multicolinearity, a positive and highly significant coefficient for variable F_t/Y_t was observed in every case. Moreover, in those cases were multicolinearity problems were absent, we also always observe positive and highly significant coefficients for variable F_t/Y_t. What is especially noteworthy, then, is the resilience of the coefficient on this borrowing variable. Even several 2SLS estimations were undertaken, and in every case the positive and significant impact of F_t/Y_t on r_{Lt} was confirmed.[6] These results are clearly quite different from the earlier studies by Makin (1983), Motley (1983), Hoelscher (1983), Mishkin (1981), Mascaro and Meltzer (1983), and Evans (1985). On the other hand, the present findings are in theory compatible with the earlier findings by Feldstein and Eckstein (1970, p. 367) that "changes in the outstanding public debt can have an important impact on the corporate bond rate."

To the extent that firms predicate investment decisions on longer term (ten-year) rates, the implications of these findings are potentially of considerable policy importance.[7] In particular, the existence of a positive, significant impact of F_t/Y_t on r_{Lt} implies the potential existence of a mechanism for the transmission of crowding out. Unlike the earlier studies, then, the present study implies a relatively greater need to come to grips with the problems of huge deficits and an enormous national debt.

On the other hand, whereas the results in this chapter cast doubt on the relevance and significance of the existing literature (which is predominantly oriented toward the nominal ninety-day Treasury bill rate), the present results are not by any means offered as definitive evidence of proof that federal borrowing in the form of ten-year U.S. government bonds acts to raise the ten-year interest rate (r_{Lt}). Such a conclusion is reasonable and very appealing but perhaps a bit premature. In particular, the kinds of models tested both here and in the already published literature may require further development, refinement, and sophistication before strong and convincing policy statements can be made. Moreover, the scope of this chapter has been restricted to the interest rate impact of sales of ten-year U.S. government bonds. Within this specific context, the empirical results imply the potential existence of a mechanism for the transmission of crowding out. However, until we can find further evidence of a similar nature for Treasury bill sales, sales of Treasury Notes, and/or sales of those long-term U.S. government bonds of more than ten years maturity,[8] it is not apparent that we have as yet established an urgent, compelling need to deal decisively and expeditiously with the deficit/debt problem.

Application of the basic model employed here to the nominal ninety-day Treasury bill rate usually fails to generate results similar to those provided above for r_{Lt}. Specifically, we have undertaken numerous estimations and have found that in nearly all cases the real value of sales of ninety-day Treasury bills (relative to real GNP) does not have a positive and significant impact on the nominal ninety-day Treasury bill rate (TR_t). In fact, the coefficient is, in most instances, negative, although generally insignificant (statistically). Typically, empirical estimations similar to the following are obtained for the nominal ninety-day Treasury bill rate:

$$TB_t = 21.212 + \underset{(+0.45)}{1.452\ TS_t/Y_t} + \underset{(+0.77)}{3.94\ [(\dot{P}_t + \dot{P}_{t-4})/2]} \quad (7.35)$$

$$- \underset{(-4.04)}{85.54\ M1_t/Y_t,}$$

$$DF = 46,\ R^2 = 0.73,\ \bar{R}^2 = 0.71,\ DW = 1.247,$$

where TS_t is the real value of sales of ninety-day Treasury bills during quarter t, expressed in annualized terms. Clearly, the coefficient in the government borrowings variable TS_t/Y_t, is negative and insignificant; this finding is consistent with most of the published literature. One possible explanation of this apparent failure of real Treasury bill sales (relative to real GNP) to influence short-term rates is that a large volume of federal government borrowings may lead investors to expect inflation to occur in the future but not in the more immediate future. Consequently, a large volume of federal government borrowings may not lead investors to demand an inflation premium (that is, a higher yield) on short-term loans to the Treasury. Alternatively, of course, a Federal Reserve Open Market policy involving only, principally, or largely ninety-day Treasury bill purchases would go far to explain the apparent insensitivity of TB_t to variable TS_t/Y_t.

In closing, it is clear that total federal borrowing in a given period essentially consists of two forms of borrowing: (1) borrowing to cover the period's federal budget deficit; and (2) borrowing to cover refinancing of the period's maturing federal debt. Clearly, if a federal budget deficit somehow acts, ceteris paribus, to elevate interest rates, but ceteris paribus does not hold, then the interest rate effects of the federal deficit could be either exacerbated (if the rate of borrowing for refinancing purposes in that period accelerates measurably) or diminished or totally offset (if the rate of borrowing for refinancing purposes decelerates measurably).

In addition, there is also the issue of state plus local government finances to be considered. In other words, in a given period, total borrowing by all levels of government consists of: (1) borrowing to cover the period's federal budget deficit; (2) borrowing to cover refinancing of the period's maturing federal debt; and (3) net borrowing by all state and local governments combined. Obviously, if state plus local governments as a whole should be, in a given period, in a budgetary surplus, and if a federal budget deficit somehow acts, ceteris paribus, to elevate interest rates, the surplus in question could partially (or even totally) offset the interest rate effects of the deficit in question.

Thus, what this chapter suggests is that empirical studies of the effects of federal deficits may need to account for government borrowing beyond that which occurs simply to directly finance those federal deficits. In other words, studies of the impact of federal deficits may need to account for either aggregate state and local government budgetary considerations or federal refinancing operations (or both).

Indeed, it may be appropriate to allow for one or both of these alternative considerations not only when examining the possibility of a transmission mechanism for crowding out, but also when attempting to measure the magnitude of crowding out. In the latter vein, Cebula (1985) has in fact recently found evidence of partial crowding out, even after allowing for the aggregate budget surplus (or deficit) of state and local governments. This finding is consistent with earlier studies by Abrams and Schmitz (1978), Arestis (1979), and Zahn (1978), all finding evidence of partial crowding out.

Notes

1. F_t includes all federal government borrowings in the form of ten-year U.S. government bonds, both for on-budget as well as off-budget items.

2. This finding, relative to the impact of the expected inflation variable ($\dot{P}_t$ $\dot{P}_{t-4}$)/2, difers from that in Mishkin (1981), who finds the actual, lagged rate of inflation to have a negative and statistically significant impact on the real rate of interest. The difference between the present results and those by Mishkin are at least in part attributable to the fact that Mishkin deals with the real rate of interest, whereas we deal with the nominal rate of interest.

3. The studies by Carlson (1977), Hoelscher (1983), and Tanzi (1970) suggest the use of the unemployment rate rather than $\dot{Y}_t$. If in this general model we use the unemployment rate in lieu of $\dot{Y}_t$ the overall results are materially the same as shown in equations 7.16 and 7.17. For example, if we use $UNEMP_t$, defined here as the unemployment rate (seasonally adjusted) of the civilian labor force in quarter t, in place of $\dot{Y}_t$ in equation 7.17, the OLS results become

$$r_{Lt} = 14.408 + \underset{(+4.20)}{29.686\ F_t/Y_t} + \underset{(+2.47)}{1.56\ [(\dot{P}_t + \dot{P}_{t-4})/2]}$$

$$- \underset{(-0.80)}{0.15\ \text{UNEMP}_T} - \underset{(-2.78)}{36.98\ (M1_{t-4}/Y_{t-4})},$$

$$DF = 45, \quad R^2 = 0.76, \quad \bar{R}^2\ 0.74, \quad DW = 1.32, \quad S = 1.047.$$

The results shown here are much the same as those shown in equation 7.17. It should be noted that substituting UNEMP_t for $\dot{Y}_t$ in equation 7.16 also generates results very similar to those reported in equation 7.16. Observe, then, the continued significance of the positive coefficient on variable F_t/Y_t. Naturally, multicolinearity (severe) precludes using $\dot{Y}_t$ and UNEMP_t together in the same regression.

4. For example, the following two-equation system was estimated by 2SLS:

$$r_{Lt} = j_{0t} + j_1(F_t/Y_t) + j_2[\dot{P} + \dot{P}_{t-4}))/2] + j_3 r_{Lt-1}$$
$$+ j_4(M1_t/Y_t) + \mu^*$$

$$(F_t/Y_t) = k_{0t} + k_{1t} r_{Lt} + k_2 \dot{Y}_t + K_3 \text{UNEMP}_t + \mu^{**},$$

where UNEMP_t is the unemployment rate (seasonally adjusted) of the civilian labor force in quarter t; j_{0t}, k_{0t} equals constant terms; and μ^*, μ^{**} equals stochastic error terms.

5. For example, the unemployment rate of the civilian labor force has been used in place of $\dot{Y}_t$. In addition, M_{t-2}/Y_{t-2} has been used in place of M_t/Y_t and $M_{t-4}/Y_{t/4}$. Furthermore, $\dot{Y}_{t-1}$, $\dot{Y}_{t-2}$, and $\dot{Y}_{t-4}$ have all been used in place of $\dot{Y}_t$. Finally, a distributed lag form of expected inflation function has been used in place of $(\dot{P}_t + \dot{P}_{t-4})/2$, as has the simple variable $\dot{P}_{t-4}$ by itself. Consider, for example, the following OLS results:

$$r_{Lt} = +12.22 + \underset{(+2.92)}{1.7306\ \dot{P}_{t-4}} + \underset{(+2.02)}{0.0563\ \dot{Y}_{t-4}} + \underset{(+3.49)}{27.239\ F_t/Y_t}$$

$$- 31.78\ M1_{t-4}/Y_{t-4},$$

$$DF = 45, \quad R^2 = 0.81, \quad \bar{R}^2 = 0.79, \quad DW = 1.86, \quad S = 1.99.$$

Note again the significant positive coefficient on variable F_t/Y_t.

6. It should be noted that the real long-term rate, defined here as r_{Lt} minus the actual inflation rate (of the CPI), has also been found to be significantly (and positively) determined by variable F_t/Y_t. This is illustrated in the following OLS estimation:

$$(r_{Lt} - \dot{P}_t) = 3.856 + \underset{(+7.37)}{29.194\ F_t/Y_t} + \underset{(+0.51)}{0.01\ \dot{Y}_t} + \underset{(+7.30)}{0.42\ TR_t},$$

$$DF = 46, \quad R^2 = 0.85, \quad \bar{R}^2 = 1.03, \quad S = 1.062.$$

Several alternative regression specifications have also been estimated for the variable $(r_{Lt} = \dot{P}_t)$, including a number of two-equation systems estimated by 2SLS. In each instance, the coefficient on variable F_t/Y_t is both positive and statistically significant.

7. Of course, the potential importance of the empirical findings in this paper regarding the impact of F_t/Y_t on r_{Lt} is all the more enhanced when one considers the highly significant impact of U.S. interest rates the value of the U.S. dollar in international markets.

8. Results quite similar to those shown here for ten-year U.S. government bonds have also been derived for the case of twenty-year U.S. government bonds.

References

Abrams, B.A., and M.D. Schmitz, 1978. The "Crowding Out" Effect of Government Transfers on Private Charitable Contributions, *Public Choice,* vol. 33, pp. 29–39.

Anderson, C.L., and J.L. Jordan, 1968. Monetary and Fiscal Actions: A Test of Their Relative Importance in Economic Stabilization, *Federal Reserve Bank of St. Louis Review,* November, pp. 11–24.

Arestis, P., 1979. "The Crowding Out" of Private Expenditure by Fiscal Actions: An Empirical Investigation, *Public Finance/Finances Publiques,* vol. 34, pp. 19–41.

Barth, J.R., G. Iden, and F.S. Russek, 1985. Federal Borrowing and Short Term Interest Rates: Comment, *Southern Economic Journal,* vol. 50, pp. 554–559.

Carlson, J.A., 1977, A Study of Price Forecasts, *Annals of Economic and Social Measurement,* vol. 16, pp. 27–56.

Cebula, R.J., 1985. Crowding Out and Fiscal Policy in the United States: A Note on the Recent Experience, *Public Finance/Finances Publiques,* vol. 40, pp. 133–136.

Cebula, R.J., C. Carlos, and J.M. Koch, 1981. The "Crowding Out" Effect of Federal Government Outlay Decisions: An Empirical Note, *Public Choice,* vol. 36, pp. 329–336.

Evans, P., 1985. Do Large Deficits Produce High Interest Rates? *American Economic Review,* vol. 75, pp. 68–87.

Feldstein, M., and O. Eckstein, 1970. The Fundamentals Determinants of the Interest Rate, *Review of Economics and Statistics,* vol. 52, pp. 363–375.

Gibson, W.E., 1970. Price-Expectations on Interest Rates, *Journal of Finance,* vol. 25, pp. 19–34.

Hoelscher, G., 1983. Federal Borrowing and Short Term Interest Rates, *Southern Economic Journal,* vol. 50, pp. 319–333.

Keran, M.W., 1969. Monetary and Fiscal Influences on Economic Activity—The Historical Evidence, *Federal Reserve Bank of St. Louis Review,* November, pp. 5–24.

Keran, M.W., 1970. Monetary and Fiscal Influences on Economic Activity: The Foreign Experience, *Federal Reserve Bank of St. Louis Review,* February, pp. 16–28.

Makin, J.H., 1983. Real Interest, Money Surprises, Anticipated Inflation and Fiscal Deficits, *Review of Economics and Statistics,* vol. 65, pp. 374–384.

Mascaro, A., and A.H. Meltzer, 1983. Long- and Short-Term Interest Rates in a Risky World, *Journal of Monetary Economics,* vol. 10, pp. 485–518.

Mishkin, F.S., 1981. The Real Interest Rate: An Empirical Investigation, *Carnegie-Rochester Conference Series on Public Policy,* pp. 151–200.

Motley, B., 1983. Real Interest Rates, Money, and Government Deficits, *Federal Reserve Bank of San Francisco, Economic Review,* Summer, pp. 31–45.

Patinkin, D., 1965. *Money, Interest and Prices,* 2nd ed. New York: Harper & Row.

Sullivan, B.P., 1976. Crowding Out Estimated From Large-Scale Econometric Model, *Federal Reserve Bank of Dallas, Business Review,* June, pp. 1–7.

Tanzi, V., 1970. Inflationary Expectations, Economic Activity, Taxes, and Interest Rates, *American Economic Review,* vol. 70, pp. 12–21.

Yohe, W.P., and D.S. Karnosky, 1969. Interest Rates and Price Level Changes, 1952–69, *Federal Reserve Bank of St. Louis Review,* December, pp. 18–38.

Zahn, F., 1978. A Flow of Funds Analysis of Crowding Out, *Southern Economic Journal,* vol. 45, pp. 195–206.

8
Controlling the Deficit: The Constitutional Amendment Approach

There is conflicting evidence as to the impacts of federal budget deficits. The conflicting evidence involves the following: (1) as indicated by the analysis in chapter 7, the identity of the mechanism or mechanisms through which the deficit impacts on the economy; (2) whether the deficit actually results in negative economic consequences; and (3) the extent (if any) to which negative economic consequences result from the deficit.

On the other hand, although there are still a number of dissenters, most policymakers seemingly agree that something must be done to control the size of the federal budget deficit. There appear to be a number of possible general means for dealing with the deficit, including the following: tax reform, tax increases, cuts in defense expenditures, cuts in nondefense expenditures, coordinated expansionary monetary policies, and a balanced budget amendment to the United States Constitution. Chapter 9 will briefly address certain aspects of the issues associated with the items just mentioned. Meanwhile, this chapter addresses a balanced budget amendment, an item that has received extensive attention.

Balanced Budget Amendment

The issue of a balanced budget amendment has been debated for years. This debate has, in part, contributed to the formulation of a number of possible forms for a balanced budget amendment. Most of these proposals are at least somewhat similar. Nevertheless, each proposal naturally tends to have one or more characteristics that to some degree differentiate it from the other proposals.

In order to provide the reader with a flavor for such proposals, two are presented here. These proposals, labeled below simply as Proposal A and Proposal B, are theoretically under consideration in Congress. Naturally, the ultimate form of a balanced budget amendment to the Constitution is unknown; indeed, such an amendment may never even materialize.

The version of the balanced budget amendment presented below as Proposal A was drafted some years ago. Proposal A reads as follows.[1]

Section 1. Total government outlays in any fiscal year shall not exceed the spending limit. The spending limit is equal to the average of total budget receipts in the three most recent fiscal years.

Section 2. Total government outlays include all budget and off-budget expenditures plus the present value of commitments for future outlays.

Section 3. The rate of growth of total receipts in any fiscal year shall not exceed the average rate of growth of an appropriate index in the most recently completed calendar year. The index shall be chosen by Congress and may be changed by two-thirds vote of each house.

Section 4. In the event that an emergency is declared by the president, the Congress may by two-thirds vote of each house authorize outlays for that fiscal year in excess of the spending limit.

Section 5. Congress shall enact all necessary legislation to implement the amendment.

The version of the balanced budget amendment presented below as Proposal B was introduced in the United States Senate on January 3, 1985. After being read, it was referred to the Senate's Committee on the Judiciary. Proposal B reads as follows.

Section 1. Prior to each fiscal year, the Congress shall adopt a statement of receipts and outlays for that year in which total outlays are not greater than total receipts. The Congress may amend such statement provided revised outlays are not greater than revised receipts. Whenever three-fifths of the whole number of both Houses shall deem it necessary, Congress in such statement may provide for a specific excess of outlays over receipts by a vote directed solely to that subject. The Congress and the president shall ensure, pursuant to legislation or through exercise of their powers under the first and second articles, that actual outlays do not exceed the outlays set forth in such statement.

Section 2. Total receipts for any fiscal year set forth in the statement adopted pursuant to this article shall not increase by a rate greater than the rate of increase in national income in the year or years ending not less than six months nor more than twelve months before such fiscal year, unless a majority of the whole number of both Houses of Congress shall have passed a bill directed solely to approving specific additional receipts and such bill has become law.

Section 3. Prior to each fiscal year, the president shall transmit to Congress a proposed statement of receipts and outlays for that year consistent with the provisions of this article.

Section 4. The Congress may waive the provisions of this article for any fiscal year in which a declaration of war is in effect.

Section 5. Total receipts shall include all receipts of the United States except those derived from borrowing, and total outlays shall include all outlays of the United States except those for repayment of debt principal.

Section 6. The Congress shall enforce and implement this article by appropriate legislation.

Section 7. This article shall take effect for the second fiscal year beginning after its ratification.

In principle, a balanced budget amendment is a rule that (theoretically) attempts to limit the federal government's ability to run deficits. However, exceptions appear to be possible. Witness, for example, the provisions in section 4 of Proposal A and in sections 1 and 4 of Proposal B. Such caveats are fairly commonplace in balanced budget proposals.

As appealing as balanced budget amendments may be to many policymakers, there remain major questions regarding such amendments. To begin with, it is unknown and perhaps questionable whether such an amendment will in fact ever be passed. Despite a widespread concern over the deficit, Congressional passage of one version or another of the balanced budget amendment does not seem imminent. Indeed, even if the requisite portions of both Houses of Congress should in fact pass some version of the amendment on to the states for ratification, it is unknown whether the requisite three-fourths of the states will in fact ratify it within the necessary seven-year period. Witness, for instance, the fate of the Equal Rights Amendment.

On another level, concern may be raised regarding the implications of a balanced budget amendment for the undertaking and effectiveness of traditional forms of discretionary fiscal policy. Of course, until we know the actual form of the amendment that is passed (if such an amendment is passed), we cannot address this issue rigorously. Nevertheless, it seems very likely that at least some significant limitations on the form and application of discretionary fiscal policies would be experienced under the type of amendment in question; this issue will be addressed in somewhat further detail at the end of this chapter.

Perhaps the most basic issue surrounding a balanced budget amendment is whether it can in fact even work. "Can such an amendment actually put an effective end to the pattern of federal budget deficits?" Alternatively stated, "can a rule work effectively to control the growth over time of government spending, taxes, and deficits?" That is, "is it possible to enact a rule that, if applied appropriately, can realistically be expected to reduce the growth (size) of government spending and hence, taxes and deficits?" We technically do not know whether such rules do work. Nor do we seem to know whether these are rules that can work, that is, whether such rules can be effective.

We simply cannot answer such questions with certainty. However, there exists the possibility that we can make at least some inferences on the basis of experience at the nonfederal level with tax expenditure limitations. The United States has had some experience at the nonfederal level with statutory and constitutional measures, that is, with rules attempting to control government spending and taxes at the nonfederal level. Perhaps an examination of such rules will be able to provide insights into the prospects and most fruitful forms of pursuing similar goals at the federal level via the route of a Constitutional amendment.

Most of the remainder of this chapter uses simple simulation techniques to gain insights into the potential effectiveness of using a Constitutional amendment to limit the growth of government outlays and taxation. None of the analysis below can yield truly definitive conclusions for the federal budget deficit problem. This is partly due to the nature of the simulation technique and to the fact that we do not know the form of the final version of the federal balanced budget amendment. Nevertheless, the analysis below may provide at least tentative conclusions as to the potential usefulness and potentially most useful form(s) of a balanced budget amendment. I hope this chapter will be of some interest to those concerned with controlling government spending, taxes, and deficits at the federal and nonfederal levels.

Tax Expenditure Limitations—An Initial Analysis

In 1976, New Jersey became the first state to impose a ceiling on the growth in state expenditures. The statute by which this was accomplished limited the growth in state expenditures to the growth in the state's per capita personal income.

After the approval of California's Proposition 13 in June 1978, tax limitation efforts spread quickly to other states. At the present time, seventeen states have tax expenditure limitations (TELs) in effect.[2] Moreover, this total of seventeen omits New Jersey, whose TEL expired in June 1983. Also, it omits Utah, where a TEL was passed in 1979 but, because of the failure to enact necessary supporting legislation, never went into effect.[3]

It is important to note that in no case do TELs cover the entirety of a state's revenues or expenditures. Typically, TELs do not limit expenditures that are outside of the general fund. Indeed, in a number of instances, even certain categories of spending in the general fund are ignored. Revenue sources excluded from the scope of TELs include bond revenue and federal aid.

There currently is no consensus as to the effectiveness of TELs. For example, the studies by Gold (1983) and Bails (1982) have found TELs to be largely ineffective. Similarly, Kenyon and Benker (1984, p. 438) argue that "examination of both survey results and actual expenditure data indicate that, for most states, tax or expenditure limits (TELs) have not been a constraint on growth in taxing or spending." By contrast, Shannon and Caulkins (1983) have found TELs to work effectively. For instance, Shannon and Caulkins (1983, p. 23) argue that the taxpayer's revolution of the 1978 to 1980 time period not only imposed explicit forms of tax and spending limits, but also conveyed a very powerful message to "state and local policymakers, most of whom escaped highly restrictive fiscal limitations. The message was clear: If you want to avoid Proposition 13-type restrictions, make sure that the increase in public spending does not exceed the growth of the private economy." Using a simple simulation technique, this section of the chapter examines the potential effectiveness of one form of TELs in restraining the growth of government spending and hence taxes. More specifically, this section seeks to examine the potential effectiveness of one form of TEL in slowing or reversing the growth trend in state and local government. The focus is on California's well known Proposition 4 and what the expenditure and tax effects would likely have been if Proposition 4 (or its equivalent) had been enacted in all fifty states plus the District of Columbia. The next section examines an alternative simulation based on growth of per capita personal income.

Analysis

This section examines what the government expenditure and tax burden impacts of Proposition 4 would likely (presumably) have been if it had been enacted in all of the states and the District of Columbia. Since one cannot predict with any great degree of certainty on this issue, attempts to gain insights are made by looking at the experiences of the recent past. Specifically, we first examine what happened to actual state plus local government expenditures per capita over the period fiscal year (FY) 1970 to FY1976. Next, we examine what presumably would have happened to state plus local government expenditures per capita if Proposition 4 had been in effect over the very same period. By contrasting these two sets of expenditure figures, insights into the potential impact of Proposition 4 on expenditure levels per capita (and thus on tax burdens per capita) can theoretically be gained.

Column 1 of table 8–1 provides the per capita expenditures of state plus local governments during fiscal year (FY) 1970 (July 1, 1970 to June 30, 1971). Column 2 of table 8–1 provides the per capita expenditures of state plus local governments during FY 1976 (July 1, 1976 to June 30, 1977). As the table clearly indicates, this time period—one of relatively high inflation rates in the United States—was a period of rapidly rising per capita state plus local government spending.

Table 8–1
Actual and Theoretical Per Capita Expenditure Levels, FY 1970, FY 1976
(in dollars)

State	Per Capita Expenditure 7/1/70–6/30/71 (1)	Per Capita Expenditure 7/1/76–6/30/77 (2)	Theoretical Per Capita Expenditure 7/1/76–6/30/77 (3)	Difference (2) − (3) (4)
Alabama	564	1,002	827	175
Alaska	1,828	3,275	2,680	595
Arizona	704	1,243	1,032	211
Arkansas	508	876	745	131
California	916	1,486	1,343	143
Colorado	728	1,346	1,067	279
Connecticut	790	1,152	1,158	−6
Delaware	921	1,458	1,350	108
District of Columbia	1,234	2,064	1,809	255
Florida	613	1,099	899	200
Georgia	616	1,003	903	100
Hawaii	1,126	1,915	1,651	264
Idaho	639	1,141	937	204
Illinois	711	1,266	1,042	224
Indiana	581	953	852	101
Iowa	690	1,235	1,012	223
Kansas	646	1,103	048	246
Kentucky	577	1,006	846	160
Louisiana	678	1,207	994	213
Maine	646	1,120	947	173
Maryland	780	1,453	1,144	309
Massachusetts	783	1,378	1,148	230
Michigan	757	1,390	1,110	280
Minnesota	806	1,460	1,182	278
Mississippi	595	1,018	872	146
Missouri	606	942	888	54
Montana	754	1,409	1,105	304
Nebraska	649	1,153	952	201
Nevada	956	1,470	1,402	68
New Hampshire	615	1,116	902	214
New Jersey	711	1,327	1,042	285
New Mexico	717	1,177	1,051	126
New York	1,075	1,795	1,576	219
North Carolina	527	982	773	209
North Dakota	726	1,308	1,064	244
Ohio	584	1,109	856	253
Oklahoma	623	1,045	913	132
Oregon	756	1,414	1,108	306
Pennsylvania	681	1,166	998	168
Rhode Island	687	1,283	1,007	276

Table 8–1 (continued)
(in dollars)

State	Per Capita Expenditure 7/1/70–6/30/71 (1)	Per Capita Expenditure 7/1/76–6/30/77 (2)	Theoretical Per Capita Expenditure 7/1/76–6/30/77 (3)	Difference (2) – (3) (4)
South Carolina	501	979	735	244
South Dakota	724	1,180	1,061	119
Tennessee	570	992	836	156
Texas	564	1,003	827	176
Utah	677	1,201	993	208
Vermont	840	1,280	1,232	48
Virginia	593	1,105	869	236
Washington	880	1,357	1,290	67
West Virginia	634	1,083	930	153
Wisconsin	764	1,322	1,120	202
Wyoming	940	1,572	1,378	194

Source: U.S. Bureau of the Census, 1978, table 673.

We may now consider the potential impact on state and local government spending for the same time period if Proposition 4 had been in effect in all of the fifty states plus the District of Columbia. We begin by referring to the provision in Proposition 4 that the total annual appropriations subject to limitation of the state and of each local government shall not exceed the appropriations limit of such entity of government for the prior year adjusted for changes in the cost of living and population except as otherwise provided in this Article. Hence, this measure would have limited the per capita growth in state plus local government spending in each area to the percentage increase in the cost of living (aside from population considerations).

Several observations are now in order. First, the per capita state plus local government expenditures examined in this study consist strictly of direct general expenditures of state and local governments. Included in such outlays are direct expenditures by state and local governments on education, highways, public welfare, health and hospitals, police protection, fire protection, natural resources, local parks and recreation, financial administration, sanitation, and interest on general debt. Second, it is assumed that the TEL under consideration, that is, Proposition 4, covers all direct general expenditures of state and local governments. Third, the cost of living measure that is generally accepted for the purpose of imposing an expenditure growth-rate ceiling is the consumer price index (CPI). This in fact is the precise living cost measure built into Proposition 4; hence, it is the one used in the computations below.[4] Fourth, the provision cited above sets a ceiling on most forms of state and local government spending. Hence, it is conceivable that state and local governments could increase their spending levels per capita by an amount less than the growth in the CPI.[5] Nevertheless, since there is no guarantee that they would in fact not go to the limit, in the computations provided below it is arbitrarily assumed that in each area per capita expenditures will grow by the maximum permitted under Proposition 4. Finally, it is assumed here that none of the state or local governments will invoke their so-called emergency clauses to authorize spending beyond the established ceiling.[6]

Let Mi be the maximum amount by which per capita nominal state plus local government expenditures in area i could have increased from FY 1970 to FY 1976, according to Proposition 4. To calculate Mi, we perform the following computation for each of the fifty states and the District of Columbia:

$$Mi = Ei_{(1970)} \ \Delta P_{(1970-1976)}, i = 1, \ldots, 51, \tag{8.1}$$

where $Ei_{(1970)}$ equals per capita state plus local government expenditures in area i, FY 1970; and $\Delta P_{(1970-1976)}$ equals percentage change in the CPI, FY 1970 to FY 1976. The value of $\Delta P_{(1970-1976)}$ is given by

$$\Delta P_{(1970-1976)} = \frac{171.1 - 116.7}{116.7} = 0.46615, \tag{8.2}$$

where the base year is 1967 (1967 = 100.0)

In column 3 of table 8–1, the value of Mi for each state and the District of Columbia has been added to the level of Ei for each these fifty-one areas. Therefore, the figures in column 3 represent the theoretical maximum total level per capita to which Proposition 4 would have allowed, in each individual case, state plus local government expenditures to rise over the period in question.

Column 4 shows the differences between columns 2 and 3, that is, the value of the spending level in column 2 minus that in column 3 in each case. A positive value for any given area in column 4 implies that, under Proposition 4, per capita state plus local government spending would have been lower than actually was the case.

Column 4 of table 8–1 appears to indicate that, except for Connecticut, the existence of Proposition 4 would theoretically have yielded lower per capita state plus local government spending for FY 1976. Such a conclusion may be misleading, however. The simple observation of a consistent pattern of differences does not necessarily imply that there is a statistically significant difference between the two sets of spending figures as a whole. Consequently, the next step in the analysis is to test formally whether there is in fact a statistically significant difference between the average hypothetical FY 1976 per capita government spending level under Proposition 4 and the average actual FY 1976 per capita government spending level.

We begin by stating the following test:

$$t = \frac{\bar{D}}{S_D/\sqrt{N}},$$ (8.3)

where D equals the difference in the population means; S_D equals the difference in the population standard deviations; and N equals population size. Note that the populations for columns 2 and 3 of table 8–1 are identical.

Table 8–2 provides the necessary data to make the computations in equation 8.3. Specifically, the mean actual per capita expenditure level is $1,284.49, whereas the mean theoretical per capita expenditure level is $1,086.37. The standard deviations for each of these two cases are provided in table 8–2 as well.

On the basis of the information in table 8–2, it follows that

$$\bar{D} = 1{,}284.49 - 1{,}086.37 = 198.12$$ (8.4)

and

$$S_D = 373.09 - 320.75 = 52.34.$$ (8.5)

Substituting from equations 8.4 and 8.5 into equation 8.3 yields

$$t = \frac{198.12}{52.34\sqrt{51}} = \frac{198.12}{52.34/7.14} = 27.025.$$ (8.6)

The null hypothesis is given by

$$H_o : \Delta = 0,$$ (8.7)

where Δ represents the mean difference between the actual and estimated (that is, theoretical) expenditure levels in FY 1976.

Accordingly, the t-value in equation 8.6 causes the rejection of the null hypothesis at far beyond the 99 percent confidence level. Thus, under the assumption that state and local government units would have spent up to

Table 8–2
Means and Standard Deviations
(in dollars)

	Means	*Standard Deviations*
Actual per Capita Expenditures	1,284.49	373.09
Theoretical per Capita Expenditures	1,086.37	320.75

their legal limits under Proposition 4, it has been found here that for the period studied (FY 1970 to FY 1976) the existence of a rule (in this case, Proposition 4) could have resulted in a statistically significant reduction in per capita nominal state plus local government spending. In turn, this finding is of obvious importance to taxpayers, as indicated by the provision in Proposition 4 that revenues received by an entity of government in excess of that amount appropriated by such entity in compliance with this Article during the fiscal year shall be returned by a revision of tax rates or fee schedules. Hence, the principal tax implication of the results in this section of the chapter is that for the period considered Proposition 4 could presumably have lead to a statistically significant reduction in tax levels per capita (where taxes are also measured in nominal terms).[7]

In conclusion, from this analysis of FY 1970 to FY 1976, we infer that rules (TELs) may indeed offer promise for reducing the growth rates (per capita) of both state plus local government nominal spending and state plus local government nominal tax collections. Potentially, this conclusion may lead to a degree of guarded optimism for the use of an inflation-based form of balanced budget amendment to control the federal budget. In other words, there may be reason to believe that we may be able to control the government budget by tying the hands of government officials with a Constitutional amendment using a restriction based on inflation. Such an amendment (TEL) could potentially have worked at the nonfederal level.

Tax Expenditure Limitations—An Alternative Analysis

The conclusions in the preceding section are based on a TEL that restricts the growth in per capita state plus local government spending to the inflation rate of the consumer price index. Such a basis for limiting the growth of government outlays (and hence taxes) is predicated on California's well known Proposition 4. However, it may be appropriate for us to address the possibility of restricting the growth rate in government spending to the growth rate of per capita personal income. In 1976, New Jersey enacted a statute that limited the growth in state expenditures to the growth in the state's level of per capita personal income; since 1976, a number of other states have enacted TELs having a similar basis for the limitation of government expenditure growth.

Analysis

Now we examine the impact of restricting the growth rate in per capita state plus local government spending to the growth rate in per capita personal income. The analysis in this section methodologically parallels that in the preceding section except that we use the growth rate of per capita personal income rather than the inflation rate of the consumer price index as the basis for the government spending limitation; and we use the per capita personal income growth rate for each individual area rather than the average per capita personal income growth rate for the nation as a whole.

Let Vi be the maximum amount by which per capita state plus local government spending in area i could have increased from FY 1970 to FY 1976 if Vi were limited by the growth rate in area i's per capita personal income over the same time period. To calculate Vi, $i = 1, \ldots, 51$, we perform the following calculation for each of the 50 states and the District of Columbia:

$$Vi = Ei_{(1970)}\Delta YPCi_{(1970-1976)}, \qquad (8.8)$$

where Ei represents per capita state plus local government expenditures in area i, FY 1970; and $\Delta YPCi$ represents percentage rate of change (growth) in area i's per capita personal income, 1970 to 1976. Observe that a separate calculation must be made for each of the fifty-one areas considered; furthermore, each such calculation involves each area's initial spending level (Ei) and each area's unique growth rate of per capita personal income ($\Delta YPCi$).

Column 1 of table 8–3 provides the per capita personal income in each state in 1970, and column 2 of table 8–3 provides the per capita personal income in each state for 1976. Column 3 provides the decimal corresponding to $\Delta YPCi$ for each state. Thus, column 3 provides, for each individual area, the growth rate of that area's per capita personal income over the 1970 to 1976 period.

Column 1 of table 8–4 provides the actual level of FY 1976 per capita state plus local government spending for each of the fifty-one areas studied. Based on the data in column 3, column 2 provides the theoretical level of FY 1976 per capita state plus local government expenditures for each area. The numbers shown in column 2, Ui, were computed as follows:

$$Ui = Ei + Vi = Ei(1 + \Delta YPCi), i = 1, \ldots, 51, \qquad (8.9)$$

where Ui is the theoretical total level of FY 1976 per capita state plus local government spending in area i.

Meanwhile, column 3 of table 8–4 shows the difference for each of the areas studied between the actual level and the theoretical level shown in columns 1 and 2 respectively. A positive value in column 3 indicates that the TEL under examination theoretically would have generated a reduced per capita state plus local government spending level. Conversely, a negative value in column 3 indicates that the TEL in question would theoretically have

Table 8–3
Per Capita Personal Income, FY 1970, FY 1976
(in dollars)

State	1970	1976	Growth Rate
Alabama	2,948	5,105	0.732
Alaska	4,644	10,178	1.192
Arizona	3,665	5,817	0.587
Arkansas	2,878	5,073	0.763
California	4,493	7,164	0.594
Colorado	3,855	6,503	0.687
Connecticut	4,917	7,373	0.499
Delaware	4,524	7,290	0.611
District of Columbia	5,079	8,648	0.703
Florida	3,738	6,108	0.636
Georgia	3,354	5,571	0.661
Hawaii	4,623	6,969	0.507
Idaho	3,290	5,726	0.740
Illinois	4,507	7,432	0.649
Indiana	3,772	6,257	0.659
Iowa	3,751	6,439	0.717
Kansas	3,853	6,495	0.660
Kentucky	3,112	5,423	0.743
Louisiana	3,090	5,386	0.743
Maine	3,302	5,385	0.631
Maryland	4,309	7,036	0.633
Massachusetts	4,340	6,585	0.517
Michigan	4,180	6,994	0.673
Minnesota	3,859	6,153	0.594
Mississippi	2,626	4,575	0.742
Missouri	3,781	6,005	0.588
Montana	3,500	5,600	0.600
Nebraska	3,789	6,240	0.647
Nevada	4,563	7,337	0.608
New Hampshire	3,737	5,973	0.598
New Jersey	4,701	7,269	0.546
New Mexico	3,077	5,213	0.694
New York	4,712	7,100	0.507
North Carolina	3,252	5,409	0.663
North Dakota	3,086	5,400	0.750
Ohio	4,020	6,432	0.600
Oklahoma	3,387	5,657	0.670
Oregon	3,719	6,331	0.702
Pennsylvania	3,971	6,466	0.628
Rhode Island	3,959	6,498	0.641
South Carolina	2,990	5,126	0.714
South Dakota	3,123	4,796	0.536
Tennessee	3,119	5,432	0.742
Texas	3,606	6,243	0.731
Utah	3,227	5,482	0.699

Table 8–3 (continued)
(in dollars)

State	1970	1976	Growth Rate
Vermont	3,468	5,480	0.580
Virginia	3,712	6,276	0.691
Washington	4,053	6,772	0.671
West Virginia	3,061	5,394	0.762
Wisconsin	3,812	6,293	0.651
Wyoming	3,815	6,723	0.762

Source: U.S. Bureau of the Census, 1984, table 772.

elevated that spending level. On the basis of the computations shown in table 8-4, there are a total of thirty-four positive values and sixteen negative values, with one case (Kentucky) having a zero value.[8]

Hence, it would appear that in most cases (roughly 67 percent) the TEL was seemingly effective in reducing government outlays. There were a number of cases (nearly 32 percent), however, in which the TEL was seemingly ineffective. Note also the special case of Alaska where the TEL in question would have permitted an additional $732 per capita in state plus local government spending in FY 1976. In the Alaska case it turns out there was an enormous rise (in excess of 119 percent) in per capita personal income over the period in question. In the interest of not distorting the population average and standard deviation with the inclusion of this special case, we shall exclude Alaska from the calculations and deal below with an *N* equal in size to 50.[9]

Table 8–4
Actual and Theoretical Per Capita Expenditure Levels, FY 1976
(in dollars)

State	Actual Expenditure 7/1/76–6/30/77 (1)	Theoretical Expenditure 7/1/76–6/30/77 (2)	Difference (1) – (2) (3)
Alabama	1,002	920	82
Alaska	3,275	4,007	– 732
Arizona	1,243	1,117	126
Arkansas	876	896	– 20
California	1,486	1,466	20
Colorado	1,346	1,228	118
Connecticut	1,152	1,184	– 32
Delaware	1,458	1,484	– 26
District of Columbia	2,064	2,102	– 38
Florida	1,099	1,003	96

Table 8–4 (continued)
(in dollars)

State	Actual Expenditure 7/1/76–6/30/77 (1)	Theoretical Expenditure 7/1/76–6/30/77 (2)	Difference (1) − (2) (3)
Georgia	1,003	1,023	− 20
Hawaii	1,915	1,697	218
Idaho	1,141	1,112	29
Illinois	1,266	1,172	94
Indiana	953	964	− 11
Iowa	1,235	1,185	50
Kansas	1,103	1,072	31
Kentucky	1,006	1,006	0
Louisiana	1,207	1,182	25
Maine	1,120	1,054	66
Maryland	1,453	1,274	179
Massachusetts	1,378	1,188	190
Michigan	1,390	1,266	124
Minnesota	1,460	1,285	175
Mississippi	1,018	1,036	− 18
Missouri	942	962	− 20
Montana	1,409	1,206	203
Nebraska	1,153	1,069	84
Nevada	1,470	1,537	− 67
New Hampshire	1,116	983	178
New Jersey	1,327	1,099	228
New Mexico	1,177	1,215	− 38
New York	1,795	1,620	175
North Carolina	982	876	106
North Dakota	1,308	1,271	37
Ohio	1,109	934	175
Oklahoma	1,045	1,040	5
Oregon	1,414	1,287	127
Pennsylvania	1,166	1,109	57
Rhode Island	1,283	1,122	161
South Carolina	979	859	120
South Dakota	1,180	1,112	68
Tennessee	992	993	− 1
Texas	1,003	976	27
Utah	1,201	1,150	51
Vermont	1,280	1,327	− 47
Virginia	1,105	1,003	102
Washington	1,357	1,470	− 113
West Virginia	1,083	1,117	− 34
Wisconsin	1,322	1,261	61
Wyoming	1,572	1,656	− 84

Source: U.S. Bureau of the Census, 1978, table 673.

Table 8–5
Means and Standard Deviations, Second Case
(in dollars)

	Means	*Standard Deviations*
Actual per Capita Expenditures	1,244.68	244.05
Theoretical per Capita Expenditures	1,183.41	238.50

In order to test formally the impact of the TEL in question, we once again refer to the following formulation:

$$t = \frac{\bar{D}}{S_D / \sqrt{N}}. \tag{8.10}$$

With Alaska now excluded from the analysis, table 8–5 provides the mean and standard deviations for columns 1 and 2 of table 8–4. Substituting from table 8–5 yields

$$\bar{D} = 1244.68 - 1183.41 = 61.27 \tag{8.11}$$

$$S_D = 244.05 - 238.50 = 5.55. \tag{8.12}$$

Substituting from equations 8.11 and 8.12 into equation 8.10 yields

$$t = \frac{61.27}{5.55 / \sqrt{50}} = \frac{61.27}{5.55 / 7.08} = 78.151. \tag{8.13}$$

The null hypothesis is given by

$$H_o : \Delta = 0, \tag{8.14}$$

where Δ is the mean difference between the actual and theoretical expenditure levels in FY 1976.

Clearly, the *t*-value in equation 8.13 causes the rejection of the null hypothesis at far beyond the 99 percent confidence level. The implications of this form of TEL for controlling the growth of per capita government spending (and taxes) are similar to those already presented at the end of the preceding section of this chapter.

At least three closing remarks are now in order. First, both forms of TEL explicitly considered here could theoretically have effectively limited the growth of government spending, at least to some degree. Second, although the two simulations examined here are very similar, they are certainly not identical. Perhaps the most important difference between the two simulations is that one simulation is tied to a single number for all areas, namely, the inflation rate of the consumer price index nationally, whereas the other simulation is tied to a different number for each area, namely, the growth rate of that particular area's per capita personal income. Third (although not presented here), a number of regressions have been estimated to test the effectiveness of TELs. Using a dummy variable to indicate the presence or absence of a TEL, most of these regressions indicate that TELs had a reasonably significant negative impact on the growth rate of per capita real state plus local government spending from 1977 to 1981.

Federal Case: Applying the TELs

For the period FY 1970 to FY 1976, let us now examine what would presumably have been the effect on the federal budget of (1) a TEL limiting the growth rate of per capita federal government spending to the inflation rate of the consumer price index, and (2) a TEL limiting the growth rate of per capita federal government spending to the growth rate of per capita personal income. We shall also consider a third rule in this section.

The first problem to be addressed is that of determining the scope of federal government spending to be placed under the limitation. Clearly, this will ultimately depend on the final form of the balanced budget amendment that is enacted (if such an amendment is enacted). On the basis of balanced budget Proposal A, total federal government outlays would include all budget and off-budget expenditures plus the present value of commitments for future outlays. On the basis of Proposal B, total federal government outlays would include all outlays of the United States except those for repayment of the national debt principal.

For simplicity, we define the federal government outlays to be subject to limitation as consisting of all budget outlays plus all off-budget outlays. For FY 1970 and FY 1976, table 8–6 provides the actual levels of total federal government outlays so defined.[10] Table 8–6 also provides the actual levels of per capita federal outlays for FY 1970 and FY 1976. Using the inflation factor provided in equation 8.2 of 0.46615, table 8–6 provides the theoretical per capita level of federal government outlays resulting from the *inflation method,* that is, the restricting of the growth rate of per capita government spending to the inflation rate of the consumer price index. As table 8–6 shows, application of the TEL method of limiting the growth rate of per capita federal outlays to the inflation rate of the consumer price index seems to reduce total federal spending in FY 1976 by 66.2 billion current dollars.

In table 8–7, we apply the *per capita income method* form of TEL, that is, the restricting of the growth rate of per capita government outlays to the

Table 8-6
Total and Per Capita Federal Outlays

	FY 1970	FY 1976
Actual Federal Outlays (in billions of current dollars)	195.7	371.8
Actual per Capita Federal Outlays (in current dollars)	960.02	1,712.61
Theoretical per Capita Federal Outlays, Inflation Method (in current dollars)	—	1,407.53
Theoretical Total Federal Outlays, Inflation Method (in billions of current dollars)	—	305.6
Theoretical Net Reduction in Total Federal Outlays, Inflation Method (in billions of current dollars)	—	66.2

Source: U.S. Bureau of the Census, 1984, table 498.

Table 8-7
Pattern of Total and Per Capita Federal Outlays

	FY 1970	FY 1976
Actual Federal Outlays (in billions of current dollars)	195.7	371.8
Actual per Capita Federal Outlays (in current dollars)	960.02	1,712.61
Theoretical per Capita Federal Outlays, Per Capita Income Method (in current dollars)	—	1,546.59
Theoretical Total Federal Outlays, Per Capita Income Method (in billions of current dollars)	—	335.8
Theoretical Net Reduction in Total Federal Outlays, Per Capita Income Method (in billions of current dollars)	—	36.0

Source: U.S. Bureau of the Census, 1984, table 498.

percentage growth rate of per capita personal income. Per capita personal income in the United States as a whole grew by 61.1 percent from 1970 to 1976. Table 8-7 shows that if the growth rate of per capita total federal government outlays is limited to the growth rate of per capita personal income, then the theoretical per capita level of total federal outlays in FY 1976 is reduced from $1,712.61 to $1,546.59. This reduction in turn translates into a theoretical net reduction in the total federal outlays in FY 1976 of 36.0 billion current dollars.

In tables 8-6 and 8-7, we have considered the theoretical impact of two possible forms of TEL on total federal outlays for FY 1970 to FY 1976. In each case, it appeared that the strict application of the TEL in question achieved a noticeable reduction in total federal outlays.[11] This conclusion parallels that obtained earlier for these same two forms of TEL. The reader may verify that the strict application of either of the two forms of TEL in question through the current time period would have generated the same basic conclusion.[12] Moreover, our basic conclusion also is sustained for most alternative definitions of the federal outlays to be limited by the TELs in question.

Of course, there are alternatives to the inflation method and the per capita income method. One such alternative would be to limit the rate of growth in total federal government outlays to the rate of growth of national income. In effect, this rule is consistent with section 2 of balanced budget Proposal B. Table 8–8 provides actual and theoretical levels of total federal government outlays for FY 1970, FY 1976, and, to be more current, FY 1982. As shown in the table, this rule of limiting the growth rate in total federal spending to the growth rate of national income would apparently have yielded a theoretical reduction in total federal outlays of 38.5 billion current dollars in FY 1976 and a theoretical reduction of 76.8 billion current dollars in FY 1982.

Concluding Remarks

This chapter has attempted to provide insights to help determine whether rules intended to control the growth of government spending and, hence, taxes can theoretically work. Ultimately, of course, the concern is over whether, through the control of government spending and taxes, a balanced budget amendment to the United States Constitution could theoretically achieve its alleged objective.

Perhaps the most basic question we must address is whether rules intended to control the growth of government spending and, hence, taxes can theoretically work. On the basis of our two simulations involving per capita state and local government spending and our three essentially parallel but briefer simulations involving total federal government spending or per capita total federal government spending, it would seem that such rules potentially can be successful. That is, such rules, if applied strictly, theoretically can act to reduce the growth of government spending. Moreover, although not examined here, other rules can be shown to be potentially effective as well.

The next basic question we address is, given that at least certain specific rules theoretically can succeed at reducing the growth of government spending, under what circumstances will they fail to do so. To start, it is clear that the choice of rule is critical. That is, if government spending growth is somehow limited by the growth of a factor that grows much more rapidly than, say, per capita personal income, then government spending growth either could exceed existing patterns or simply could fail to be significantly reduced.

Table 8–8
Pattern of Total Federal Outlays

	FY 1970	FY 1976	FY 1982
Actual Total Federal Outlays (in billions of current dollars)	195.7	371.8	745.7
Theoretical Total Federal Outlays (in billions of current dollars)	—	333.3	668.9
Theoretical Reduction in Total Federal Outlays (in billions of current dollars)	—	38.5	76.8
National Income (in billions of current dollars)	798.4	1,359.8	2,446.8

Source: U.S. Bureau of the Census, 1984, table 498.

A more significant threat to the potential effectiveness of rules is the emergency clause. Such a clause is explicitly included in section 4 of Proposal A. Moreover, exceptions or escape clauses are found in sections 1 and 4 of Proposal B. Such emergency clauses, exceptions clauses, and escape clauses are a common feature of TELs and of proposed balanced budget amendments.

It is possible that even a recession, particularly if severe, could constitute an emergency or exception. Indeed, the word *emergency* can be interepreted to apply to a range of possible circumstances. Accordingly, such clauses could convert a balanced budget amendment into useless rhetoric. Concern on this point is expressed by Bails (1982, p. 138) who, after analyzing a TEL in Arizona, alleges that "escape clauses give political decision makers a device by which the limitation can be exceeded with relative ease."

Assuming that a rule is established and well chosen, strictly applied, and emergency clauses are not abused, the federal budget should generally be balanced even during times of recession. To some degree, then, fiscal policy loses flexibility to cope with the business cycle. Moreover, the debilitating effects of the rule may not be restricted to discretionary fiscal policy. The economy possesses automatic stabilizers, such as the income tax and unemployment compensation, which change automatically in response to the economy. As a result, these stabilizers tend to moderate the upturns and downturns that the economy experiences over the course of the business cycle. Consider now Proposal B. Such a rule, by requiring a balanced budget, essentially ensures that even the automatic stabilizers will be or may be neutralized since if the budget is going into deficit because of automatic stabilizers it requires (according to section 1) a three-fifths majority to permit that deficit. Otherwise taxes have to be increased or other forms of government spending must be cut. This trait of Proposal B and other such proposals is widely believed to be a major shortcoming.

In sum, then, we have used state and local data in order to provide insights as to whether a set of rules allegedly directed at slowing the growth of government spending and taxes can succeed. We have run two simulations using state and local data; each simulation corresponded to an actually enacted state constitutional amendment or statute. In each case, we determined that such a rule theoretically could have successfully reduced state plus local government spending (and hence state plus local government taxes). These findings thus created an optimism that, in theory, rules to limit government spending (and taxes) can work. Applying these same two rules, plus a third rather similar rule, to the federal budget generated the same basic conclusion. Accordingly, we infer that such rules may be useful to the pursuit of a balanced federal budget.

While those interested in state and local government finances as well as those interested in a balanced budget amendment may view these findings as relevant, they must not lose sight of the potentially adverse impact of emergency clauses, escape clauses, and exception clauses in any rule that might be established. Finally, we must also be cognizant of the negative implications at the federal level of any rule for contracyclical fiscal policy effectiveness.

Notes

1. Related to this version of the balanced budget amendment, see Aranson (1981, pp. 671–672).

2. These TELs are different from the Rainy Day Funds (RDFs), which are merely contingency funds. RDFs are found in nineteen states.

3. As Gold (1984, p. 422) notes, "Eight TELs are constitutional, and the rest are set forth in statutes."

4. The appropriateness of using the CPI rather than an alternative price index is not to be debated here.

5. Related to this, see the remarks by Gold (1984, p. 429).

6. Stated simply, spending growth is assumed to be restricted solely by the inflation rate of the CPI; the issue of population size (and changes therein) is not dealt with here.

7. We implicitly are assuming that there is not a significant decline or increase in the magnitude of federal aid to state and local governments. Also, by choosing to study a period prior to FY 1977, we do not study a period in which actual state plus local outlays may have been affected by the tax revolt.

8. A value of zero indicates no difference, that is, no change as a result of the TEL in question.

9. In the computations shown in tables 8–1 and 8–2, the inflation rate was uniform for all of the states. However, if the actual inflation rate in Alaska paralleled Alaska's growth rate of per capita personal income, a set of computations based on that premise would likely have required us to also extricate Alaska from our calculations in table 8–2 and equations 8.4, 8.5, and 8.6.

10. These figures do include off-budget outlays.

11. In the case of state and local governments the existence of means and standard deviations enables us to formally test for statistically significant differences in those means. No such comparison is technically possible in the federal case, however.

12. Implicitly, we are ignoring emergency clauses, escape clauses, and exceptions clauses. These items are discussed later in this chapter.

References

Aranson, P.H., 1981. *American Government: Strategy and Choice.* Cambridge, Mass.: Winthrop Publishers.

Bails, D., 1982. A Critique on the Effectiveness of Tax-Expenditure Limitations, *Public Choice,* vol. 38, no. 2, pp. 129–138.

Gold, S.D., 1983. *State Tax and Spending Limitations: Paper Tigers or Slumbering Giants?* Legislative Finance Paper No. 33, Denver, Colo: National Conference of State Legislatures.

Gold, S.D., 1984. Contingency Measures and Fiscal Limitations: The Real World Significance of Some Recent State Budget Innovations, *National Tax Journal,* vol. 37, no. 3, pp. 421–432.

Kenyon, D.A., and K.M. Benker, 1984. Fiscal Discipline: Lessons from the State Experience, *National Tax Journal,* vol. 37, no. 3, pp. 433–446.

Ladd, H., 1978. An Economic Evaluation of State Limitations on Local Taxing and Spending Powers, *National Tax Journal,* vol. 31, no. 1, pp. 1–18.

Ladd, H., and J.B. Wilson, 1983. Who Supports Tax Limitations: Evidence from Massachusetts Proposition 2½, *Journal of Policy Analysis and Management,* vol. 20, no. 1, pp. 256–279.

Shannon, J., and S.E. Caulkins, 1983. Federal and State-Local Spenders Go Their Separate Ways, *Intergovernmental Perspective,* vol. 8, pp. 23–29.

Shapiro, P., and W.E. Morgan, 1978. The General Revenue Effects of the California Tax Limitation Amendment, *National Tax Journal,* vol. 31, no. 2, pp. 199–228.

Stein, R.M., K.E. Hamm, and P.K. Freeman, 1983. An Analysis of Support for Tax Limitation Referenda, *Public Choice,* vol. 40, no. 2, pp. 187–194.

U.S. Bureau of the Census, 1978 and 1984. *Statistical Abstract of the United States.* Washington, D.C.: U.S. Government Printing Office.

9
Putting the Deficit in Perspective

P art III has focused on the deficit/debt issue. Chapter 6 developed the basic analytical frame of reference for understanding the crowding out phenomenon. Several possible forms of crowding out were identified and summarized. There are yet other possible forms of crowding out that could have been examined. In any event, on the basis of the theoretical literature, one potentially can infer that crowding out is complete, zero, or partial.

Chapter 7 deals with the effects of deficits (and debt) on an empirical level. It is shown that federal government borrowings act to elevate the interest rate yield on ten-year U.S. government bonds (notes). Indeed, not only was the nominal rate on these ten-year bonds found to be an increasing function of the magnitude of federal government borrowings (relative to GNP), but also the real rate on these bonds was found to be an increasing function of federal borrowings (relative to GNP). These results are compatible with an earlier study by Feldstein and Eckstein (1970) and with the following commentary by Cagan (1985, p. 205) that "The market mechanism for accommodating sources and uses of funds to an increase in federal deficits is a rise in interest rates." The results in chapter 7 indicate that this sort of interest rate outcome is to be expected. Of course, as noted earlier, this finding is at odds with a good number of other studies, including Evans (1985), Hoelscher (1983), Makin (1983), Mascaro and Meltzer (1983), and Motley (1983).

If in fact we can infer from the empirical analysis in chapter 7 that deficits do act to elevate long-term interest rates, the next issue becomes a quantitative one. And, as Cagan (1985) explains, there are at least two different views on this issue: (1) the interest rate increase will be minor; or (2) the interest rate increase will be substantial. We do not attempt to definitively resolve this issue. There will already be disagreement on the part of some that there is any significant interest rate increase at all as a result of federal borrowings (as defined)! Nevertheless, we may view the findings by Cagan (1985) of relevance here. Cagan (p. 206) finds the interest rate increase to be relatively moderate: "the actual increase . . . proved to be neither minimal nor extremely high.

If we accept this middle-of-the-road appraisal, then it would seem that we might also accept the same appraisal of crowding out. Namely, although crowding out does occur, it is definitely not complete. Later in this chapter, the discussion will argue that deficits tend to carry with them an undeniably positive net impact on aggregate output, employment, and income. This assessment of only moderate (partial) crowding out is consistent with studies by Cebula (1985), Cagan (1985), Abrams and Schmitz (1978), Arestis (1979), and Zahn (1978).

Thus, despite the great public concern over federal budget deficits the evidence implies that although there are adverse side effects from the deficits, the side effects have been only moderate. It is perhaps a bit ironic, then, that there is such a great public clamor for action to control the deficit. On the one hand, this clamor is weakly founded since there is no evidence of any catastrophic side effects from the deficit; the evidence points to negative side effects but these are moderate. Many economists are concerned that the financing and economic impacts of federal deficits appear to be somewhat unstable and that it is unclear as to how long the credit markets will be able to continue to absorb large volumes of future Treasury borrowings without greater adverse side effects. As Cagan observes, while there has been evidence of only moderate crowding out to date, this could change.

The great public clamor for deficit control has led to intensified discussion of means by which to eliminate the deficit problem. Chapter 8 dealt with the possible usefulness of a balanced budget amendment. It was argued that such a measure could potentially be useful, but such factors as emergency clauses raised significant doubts. There are, of course, alternative means by which to control the deficit. Indeed, the Gramm-Rudman-Hollings Act passed by Congress in 1985 attests to the alleged willingness of our elected officials to address the deficit problem outside the explicit arena of a Constitutional amendment. The remainder of this chapter addresses various alternatives to the Constitutional amendment approach by which to potentially control or limit the deficit. The analysis will general, the objective being simply that of highlighting certain basic issues and problems.

Tax Policy

Tax policy seems to be broken into two forms: (1) tax increases to raise revenues to lower the deficit, and (2) tax reform. In the absence of a detailed piece of actually enacted or approved legislation, it is extremely difficult (if not impossible) to definitively portray the long- or short-term effects of a policy of tax increases. Suffice it to say that, if a tax increase is enacted it can potentially act to reduce the growth of disposable income (directly or indirectly) and thus to reduce the growth of private sector spending. If this should happen, the possibility of either an economic slowdown or recession arises. Either a slowdown or recession could act to reduce the growth in actual tax collections by reducing the growth rate or size of the tax base. For example, even if a higher tax rate structure is put into effect, if it is applied to a diminished base or a more slowly growing base, lower tax collections than would originally have been collected might result. Or, alternatively, tax revenues simply may not grow by as much as was projected. In any event, given the accompanying growth in transfer payments that might be expected during an economic slowdown or recession, the deficit situation may not improve appreciably. Yet, the private sector could potentially pay a painful price for the policy experiment of raising taxes.

On the other hand, there is the case of tax reform. Obviously, given the as yet unknown final form of or effective date of the tax reform likely to be enacted, and given that a tax reform bill (if enacted) will consist of interacting parts that either offset or reinforce one another, it will be extremely difficult to project definitively the impact of the tax reform movement on any industry, firm, individual, or even the economy as a whole. Nevertheless, some general commentary and evaluation may be useful.

In terms of tax reform options, we have a number of proposals that we might discuss. Table 9–1 provides a list of better known tax reform proposals that have been put forth in recent years. The proposal called Treasury I was formally unveiled on November 27, 1984. The Reagan administration formally announced its proposal (Treasury II) on May 27, 1985. Most observers have tended to argue that the federal tax system generally changes in increments and that tax policy changes commonly reflect the demands of major special interest groups (see, for example, Reese, 1980 and Surrey (1957) and/or various politicians whose ideology involves "unobtrusively encouraging market-based, non-zero-sum economic growth" (King, 1978, p. 25). The proposals known as Treasury I and Treasury II, however, are quite different in that they propose comprehensive change unpopular with many powerful associations of special interest groups and they allegedly are targeted at achieving equity as opposed to providing capital incentives or other social goals.

In 1985, President Reagan implored Congress to follow his lead to the achievement of a reformed federal income tax system. He requested passage of Treasury II, arguing among other things that it would be essentially revenue neutral, that is, it would presumably generate the same essential revenues as current tax law over a five-year period. Note, in this time of concern over deficits and raising more tax revenues, the irony of proposing a tax reform (as opposed to an increase) that is simply (and allegedly) only revenue neutral. Of course, a reformed tax system with its presumably lower tax rates might be an easier target for politicians to take aim at if they choose to raise taxes. If a tax reform package is ultimately passed, it is likely to bear only a modest

Table 9–1
Tax Overhaul: How Various Plans Compare

1986 Tax Year	Treasury II	Current Law	Treasury I	Bradley-Gephardt	Kemp-Kasten
Individual tax rates	3 rates: 15%, 25%, 35%	14 rates from 11% to 50%	3 rates: 15%, 25%, 35%	3 rates: 14%, 26%, 30%	23% flat rate; 20% of FICA wages excluded; 20% of income exceeding FICA wages is added back
Personal exemption	$2,000	$1,080	$2,000	Taxpayer: $1,600 Dependent: $1,000 Household head: $1,800	$2,000
Mortgage interest	Principal residence deductible	Fully deductible for all mortgages	Principal residence deductible	Limited deductibility for all mortgages	Fully deductible for all mortgages
Other interest	$5,000 plus amount equal to investment income	Fully deductible	$5,000 plus amount equal to investment income	Limited deductibility of amount equal to investment income	Only for investments and education
Employer-provided health insurance	Taxed up to first $10/month for single; $25 for family	Not taxed	Taxed over $70/month for single; $175 for family	Fully taxed	Not taxed
Charitable contribution	Deductible; but only on itemized returns	Fully deductible	Deductible over 2% of gross income	Deductible only against 14% rate	Fully deductible

State and local taxes	No deduction	Fully deductible	Not deductible	Deduction for income and real property taxes; only against 14% rate	Deduction for property and sales taxes
Capital gains	50% excluded for 17.5% top rate, but fewer items covered	60% excluded for 20% top rate	Indexed for inflation; taxed as ordinary income	Taxed as ordinary income; no indexing	Either 40% excluded or indexed and taxed as ordinary income
Corporate tax rates	33% top rate, graduated rates up to $75,000	46% graduated rates up to $100,000	33% flat rate	30% flat rate	35%; graduated rates up to $100,000
Depreciation	Somewhat accelerated, but less generous than current law	Accelerated	Economic depreciation; indexed for inflation	Economic depreciation (assuming 6% inflation)	Present value of expensing

resemblance to Treasury II, although President Reagan will expect the reform package to bear at least some resemblance to the basic principles in Treasury II.

As demonstrated in table 9–1, many aspects of Treasury II would seem to be self explanatory. The current system is characterized as containing fourteen tax brackets, whereas Treasury II would involve only three tax brackets with the top rate being only 35 percent as opposed to the currently prevailing 50 percent. Whether a system with three brackets is truly a simpler system is a matter of semantics. Currently, when one computes one's taxes based on taxable income, it is unnecessary to peruse through a maze of fourteen different tax rates. The process of determining taxable income is difficult; after completing the task, however, the effort to compute the tax liability is very simple. The personal exemption under Treasury II is raised from its current level of $1,080 to $2,000. The problem with this aspect of the tax reform is that it not only is not a simplification for taxpayers (except those who are thereby dropped from the tax rolls) but it also leads to a potentially significant loss of tax revenue. Depending on whose forecast one listens to, this aspect of Treasury II would cut tax revenues annually by up to 40 billion dollars. A tax credit in lieu of this tax deduction could easily be constructed so that it still would permit dropping low income taxpayers from the tax rolls, but it would sharply reduce the tax revenue loss.

While some reduction in the number of tax brackets, a reduction in the top tax rate, and a near doubling of the personal exemption are realistically to be included in the tax reform package that may ultimately be enacted, there are a number of aspects of Treasury II that are likely to survive. One of these involves the deductibility of state and local taxes. Under current law, such items are fully deductible on itemized returns. By contrast, under Treasury II, no deduction would be permitted for these items. For states where state plus local taxes are relatively high and where taxpayers on the average also have relatively high incomes so that they are relatively likely to itemize their deductions, this could present a number of problems. For example, in such high tax states, taxpayers may suffer a disproportionately higher effective tax burden from tax reform than they would if they were to reside in relatively lower tax states. Obviously, this presents potential problems on equity grounds. In addition, on the basis of a number of empirical studies such as those by Pack (1973), Cebula (1974), and Ostrosky (1978) there may be longer-term implications in terms of geographic mobility. People may choose to relocate in lower tax areas. To the extent that such migration effects were manifested, there would clearly be economic ramifications in terms both of the geographic redistribution of long-term economic growth and state plus local government finance and resource problems. Moreover, cities, counties, and states may experience growing political pressure to reduce taxes (or at least to curtail the growth in taxes). This pressure is of course especially likely in those areas where the tax levels are relatively higher. This pressure may then mandate some curtailing of public services.[1] Aside from the direct utility losses resulting from the latter curtailment, there are obvious threats to employment in the nonfederal public sector. These various political considerations, combined with the aforementioned equity and migration (economic) considerations, make the Treasury II proposal in this case unpalatable in its strict form. An alternative might be a compromise where state and local income taxes (and probably property taxes) remain deductible on itemized returns, but other state and local taxes lose deductibility.[2]

Next, for the individual, the exclusion for net capital gains would be reduced from 60 to 50 percent. The top effective rate on capital gains would be reduced to 17.5 percent, given the proposed top rate on ordinary income of 35 percent. The impact of the proposals as a whole, however, reduces the differential between ordinary income and capital assets dramatically. Under current law, a $1,000 investment return is worth, on an after-tax basis, either $500 or $800 to a top-bracket taxpayer depending on whether it is capital or ordinary. Thus, capital gain treatment increases after-tax income by 60 percent. Under the proposal that same $1,000 investment return will be worth $650 or $825 after-tax basis. The increase in after-tax income attributable to capital gain status is only 27 percent.

Gains from the sale, disposition, or conversion of depreciable or depletable property placed in service (on or after a given date) that is used in a trade or business would no longer be eligible for capital gains treatment. The basis of these assets would, however, be indexed for depreciation or depletion purposes. This proposal could have a major negative impact on real estate transactions which, in the past, could be planned to avoid any ordinary income on sale of the property.

A very controversial aspect of Treasury II involves the deduction (for households) of interest payments. Treasury II would leave the home mortgage interest deduction intact for principal residences, but it would limit deductions for other interest costs including those on consumer loans and on second homes to $5,000 in excess of investment income. Thus, a taxpayer with $7,000 of investment income would be able to deduct the interest on the principal residence plus $12,000 of other interest payments.

Both interest income and interest deductions would be indexed to eliminate the effects of inflation. Each year the Treasury would announce a fraction of interest rates that may be considered the result of inflation. Taxable interest income may be reduced by that fraction, and the deduction for nonmortgage interest expense in excess of $5,000 must be reduced by the same amount.

Clearly, among other things, the financial attractiveness of second homes would be diminished. And, given the aforementioned loss of preferential capital gains treatment for real estate, construction—especially in resort areas—could suffer.

Next, consider the case of the corporate tax rates. Under Treasury II, the corporate tax rate would be graduated, with a top rate of 33 percent. By contrast, the current tax regime has the corporate tax rate graduated with a 46 percent top rate. Overall, although the corporate tax rate would be lower under Treasury II than under current law, Treasury II would allegedly raise aggregate corporate taxes by approximately $118 billion over five years. The latter revenue would offset aggregate tax reductions for individuals over the same period.

Whereas Treasury II would lower the maximum corporate income tax rate, this change would of course not help the nation's most besieged industries. For instance, the former Republic Steel Corporation, now part of the LTV Steel Company in Cleveland, has not generated any annual net income since 1981. Moreover, by lowering the corporate tax rate, Treasury II would encourage firms to raise current income and to cut back on investment in new plant and equipment.

There are other aspects of Treasury II and its treatment of corporations that are potentially disruptive to the economy. One of these is that of the investment tax credit (ITC). Started in 1981 under President Reagan's mammoth tax cut bill, the ITC allowed firms to reduce tax bills by 6 to 10 percent of the value of certain investments. Under Treasury II, the ITC would be abandoned. From the perspective of heavy manufacturers, the abandonment of the ITC may be the most onerous component of Treasury II. Many economists argue that for such industries as the steel industry, the ITC is needed to facilitate the modernization vital to offsetting the advantages of foreign competition, such as cheap labor. Potentially the loss of the ITC could have a damaging effect on heavy industry. By contrast, high-technology firms would generally not lose so heavily from the repeal of the ITC. Overall, however, to the extent that the ITC has resulted in and does result in an increased incentive to invest, its repeal could reduce the growth rate of capital formation. Ironically, in reducing the growth rate of capital formation, the repeal of the ITC conceivably could exhibit an impact similar to that of crowding out.

Treasury II also would provide somewhat accelerated, but less generous capital depreciation allowances than existing law. This would tend to some degree to exacerbate some of the effects of the repeal of the ITC. Depreciation allowances allow firms to recover capital costs over the so-called useful life of machinery or a factory. A slowdown in the depreciation schedule would act to raise the effective tax rate on income from capital goods. The less generous depreciation schedule would tend to be more burdensome to the capital-intensive firms; firms that are service oriented, high-tech, or just generally less capital intensive would also be hurt, but somewhat less, since depreciation is generally less important to them. In any event, if included in the finally enacted tax reform package, this provision of such a package would act to discourage capital formation and therefore add to the potential effects of repealing the ITC. On the other hand, the degree to which the depreciation becomes less accelerated is unknown; indeed, this provision may be, in the end, very weak.

Certainly, there are other aspects of Treasury II that may warrant some discussion. For example, it is clear that, in one way or another, Treasury II would tend to make certain financial investments more attractive and others less attractive. Many of these changes in the appeal of investment alternatives would simply result from the lower tax rate structure and/or from the new treatment of capital gains. For example, lower tax rates would make municipal bonds (which are exempt from federal income taxation) less attractive since they yield a smaller tax benefit. This fact may mandate that states and municipalities raise coupon interest rates on their bond offerings. In addition, tax shelters would lose some of their appeal because with lower tax rates, they would provide less of a tax saving. And, as already noted, the loss of preferential capital gains treatment would impact negatively on real estate.

Table 9–2 outlines some of these more attractive and less attractive financial investment alternatives. These ramifications of the tax reform, as well as others, are left to the reader to contemplate. Once the yet-to-be-passed tax bill is enacted, the actual legislation will warrant a detailed examination.

Government Spending Policies

There are of course a large number of proposals for slashing the deficit through various government spending cuts.[3] There are two major areas on

Table 9–2
Attractiveness of Investment Alternatives

More Attractive

Common stocks of companies paying high dividends
High-yielding fixed-income investments, such as corporate and Treasury bonds
Common stocks of companies with currently high effective tax rates
Mutual funds emphasizing dividend and interest income
Money market funds and bank accounts

Less Attractive

Common stocks of companies in capital-intensive industries
Tax shelters
Common stocks of companies with currently low effective tax rules
Tax-exempt securities
Common stocks of companies greatly involved with consumer lending (other than mortgages),
    retail brokerage, and fringe benefit provision, particularly insurance
Mutual funds emphasizing capital grain distribution
Real estate, especially in vacation areas
Other tangible assets, such as collectibles, assuming continued low inflation
Annuities and some other tax deferment vehicles

which most such proposals focus: defense spending and domestic (nondefense) spending. We shall briefly discuss defense spending first and then refer to nondefense spending and Congressional spending cuts.

According to the Congressional Budget Office (CBO), appropriations requests by the Reagan Administration for national defense programs will rise from $323 billion in budget authority in FY 1986 to $488 billion in budget authority in FY 1990, for a five-year total of about $2 trillion. Of course, these are budget requests and are thus subject to all of the impacts of the political process, including the impact of the 1985 Gramm-Rudman-Hollings Act, to be discussed shortly.

In certain respects, it may be helpful to view the defense budget as a large pie to be cut into 50 slices, one for each state. For an idea of the size of those slices refer to table 9–3. Table 9–3 indicates FY 1985 defense spending in each of the states on two bases: total current dollar outlays in each state and per capita current dollar outlays in each state. As shown, California received the largest share of the total defense spending ($41.0 billion), whereas Virginia received the highest per capita level of defense spending ($2,437.00).

Table 9–3 implies that the defense budget is very unevenly distributed among the 50 states, both in terms of total dollar outlays and on a per capita basis. Thus, certain states would appear to have a far greater stake in the size and disposition of the defense budget than others. Politically, this translates into vehement opposition in Congress on the part of a number of states, many of which have large populations and a correspondingly large representation in the House, to defense cutbacks.

As for nondefense spending, emotions run high on a broad spectrum of programs. Nondefense outlays involve such diverse expenditures as those for income security; health; veterans benefits and services; education, training, and employment; social security and medicare; natural resources and the environment; energy; agriculture; community and regional development; science, space, and technology; the administration of justice; mass transit; highways; housing assistance; and international affairs. The political web in which Congressmen, Congresswomen, and Senators find themselves is indeed very tangled and complex. Inertia to change is predictable; inertia for reductions in specific programs is also predictable, perhaps more so.

In the face of various forms of powerful resistance to reductions in both defense outlays and nondefense outlays, can the Gramm-Rudman-Hollings Act (and its presumed underlying philosophy of pursuing deficit reduction) really work? Can the Gramm-Rudman-Hollings Act, with its various provisions for automatically reducing the federal deficit, really work to restore what some refer to as fiscal responsibility? It is possible, but it seems most unlikely.

Our Congressmen, Congresswomen, Senators, and President are well aware that numerous programs have outlived their basic function and that

Table 9–3
Total and Per Capita Defense Spending, FY 1985

State	Total Spending (billions of dollars)	Per Capita Spending (dollars)
Virginia	13.9	2,437
Hawaii	2.6	2,429
Alaska	1.2	2,215
Connecticut	6.1	1,917
Missouri	8.8	1,750
Maryland	7.1	1,608
California	41.0	1,555
Massachusetts	8.6	1,471
Washington	6.0	1,351
Kansas	2.9	1,202
Maine	1.3	1,138
New Hampshire	1.1	1,083
Georgia	6.3	1,061
Texas	16.5	1,006
Utah	1.6	986
Arizona	3.1	983
Colorado	3.1	945
New Mexico	1.3	874
Florida	9.7	856
Mississippi	2.2	851
Alabama	3.2	794
Rhode Island	0.8	793
South Carolina	2.6	789
Delaware	0.5	729
Indiana	4.0	719
Louisiana	3.2	707
New Jersey	5.3	706
North Dakota	0.5	705
Oklahoma	2.1	651
New York	11.3	638
Minnesota	2.6	614
North Carolina	3.8	613
Ohio	6.3	589
Arkansas	1.4	582
Nevada	0.5	554
Pennsylvania	6.4	536
Wyoming	0.3	507
Kentucky	1.7	465

Table 9–3 continued

State	Total Spending (billions of dollars)	Per Capita Spending (dollars)
Nebraska	0.7	438
Vermont	0.2	414
Michigan	3.6	396
South Dakota	0.3	359
Tennessee	1.6	329
Montana	0.3	323
Illinois	3.4	295
Wisconsin	1.4	293
Idaho	0.3	273
Iowa	0.7	260
Oregon	0.6	220
West Virginia	0.2	126

they should consequently be terminated. Nevertheless, the political process has resulted in few terminations. Indeed, the *President's Private Sector Survey on Cost Control* (Grace Commission, 1984, p. 5) "found Congressional interference to be a problem. For example, because Congress obstructs the closing of bases that (even) the military wants to close, the three-year waste is $367 million." The President, for all of his rhetoric in favor of spending cuts, has provided only a modicum of actual cuts. It has been during his terms in office that aggregate federal spending and deficits (in nominal and real terms) have risen so rapidly. Although Reagan attempts to place the blame on Congress, the actual facts do not entirely support his allegations. Congress has allocated more for social programs than the President wanted; however, Congress has simultaneously allocated less for defense spending. The result is that, say, for the period FY 1982 through FY 1984, Congress spent about $60 billion above the aggregate budget requested by the President. And that $60 billion represents only 11.5 percent of the aggregate budget deficits accumulated for those same three fiscal years.

Moreover, Reagan has frequently failed to exercise his veto power to reduce spending. For the period 1981 through 1985, he vetoed only forty-five bills, an average of nine per year. By contrast, President Ford used his veto an average of twenty-two times per year, and President Truman an average of fifty times per year.

In 1981, Reagan successfully obtained Congressional approval of over $35 billion in spending cuts. Subsequent efforts at such deep cuts have failed. It may be that when Congress is voting on individual programs all it directly feels is the pressure from special interest groups. Perhaps Congress feels no simultaneous and consistent offsetting pressure from taxpayers.

Moreover, Congress and the President have always liked to play number games. These number games take a variety of forms. One form involves announcing that one has achieved a savings of X billions of dollars on a program, when in reality if an investigation is undertaken, it can be shown that spending within the program in question has actually risen by Y billions of dollars over the previous year's level. Why can politicians get away with such misleading rhetoric? The approved program is actually X billions of dollars less than the initial budget request!

But there are more misleading forms of number games that politicians play. One of the most deceptive is that of inflating estimates of needed spending and/or of expected revenues. Committee chairpersons commonly submit inflated estimates of spending needs to the budget committee since each of these committee chairpersons generally wants to maximize his/her committee's allocation. Moreover, the budget committee itself is culpable of intentionally inflating or deflating: it frequently underestimates certain categories of outlays and overestimates expected revenue receipts. The outcome can be approval of a relatively meaningless budget resolution.

And what if the President refuses to play along with Congress's budget games? In 1972, Nixon decided to impound funds appropriated by the Congress. In response to this course of action, Congress legislated the Congressional Budget and Impoundment Control Act of 1974. This legislation restricted impoundment, established budget committees in both the Senate and the House, and mandated annual budget resolutions that presumably would act to set a ceiling on aggregate federal government spending. There were, ostensibly, two objectives to the legislation: (1) to create a greater degree of control over the budget for Congress; and (2) to help constrain the level and growth of federal government expenditures. Clearly, the Congressional Budget and Impoundment Control Act of 1974 has been an utter failure in controlling the growth of federal spending. For example, federal outlays grew from 267.9 billion current dollars in FY 1974 to nearly a trillion current dollars in FY 1986. Even after adjusting for inflation, real federal outlays have grown enormously over this relatively brief period. Moreover, the federal deficit rose from 4.7 billion current dollars in FY 1974 to roughly 180 billion current dollars in FY 1986 (and 211.9 billion current dollars in FY 1985).

It is perhaps interesting to note that in the context of the Congressional Budget and Impoundment Control Act of 1974, Congress chose to expressly protect such entitlements as veterans benefits and Medicare. Moreover, Congress turned down a "rule of consistency." Such a rule would have required spending increases in a given program to be offset elsewhere.

Theoretically, the Gramm-Rudman-Hollings Act is meant to deal directly and strongly with the deficit problem. This legislation provides a blueprint for cutting the deficit over a five-year period, down to zero by 1991. According to the Gramm-Rudman-Hollings Act, if the deficit is not cut or cut sufficiently by Congress (and the President), then automatic budget reductions will occur, in an across-the-board fashion.

At first, this legislation appeared to have generated an extraordinarily powerful pressure to cut outlays and, possibly, to even elevate taxes. But, the Act already is in the courts on constitutional grounds. If that does not kill the initiative, then we should not be altogether shocked if Congress overrides the Act—which Congress can, by a simply majority vote.

As a possible index of things to come, consider the fact that a mere one- or two-year freeze on cost-of-living adjustments (COLAs) to Social Security could easily trim tens and tens of billions from the federal budget over the next five years. Yet, at the behest of President Reagan, Social Security was exempted from the Gramm-Rudman-Hollings Act.

It would appear that Congress's (and the President's) capacity for self control is extremely limited. Although the Gramm-Rudman-Hollings Act may bring a temporary slowdown in the growth of federal spending and deficits, there appears to be little reason to believe that, one way or another, the impact of this legislation on the federal budget will not be very short lived.

But what if sizable spending cuts are in fact involved? There is a potential danger just as there was a potential danger with tax increases. Namely, depending on the magnitude, nature, and timing of such spending cuts, either an economic slowdown or a recession could potentially result. Ironically, the theoretical gains toward deficit reduction could then be partially or even totally offset by reduced tax collections and expanded government transfers. If a policy of spending cuts, or perhaps more accurately, reduced spending growth, is undertaken, our decision makers need to be cautious as to the form, size, and timing of those cuts if they are to effectively pursue deficit reduction. Recession and/or a larger deficit problem could potentially arise.

Monetary Policy

A brief mention of the potential role of monetary policy may be in order. If a coordinated effort between monetary policy decision makers and fiscal decision makers occurs, it would seem at least plausible for progress toward deficit reduction to be made with a relative minimum of adverse effects to the economy as a whole.

Potentially, an effectively executed, expansionary monetary policy could be combined with a very cautious, moderate policy of deficit reduction by the Congress and the President. With monetary expansion, if it is sufficiently strong, interest rates could be pushed downward. In turn, consumer spending and investment spending would presumably rise, pushing upward on the GNP level. The latter impact would in turn act to elevate tax collections (and perhaps to reduce government transfers). With downward pressure on interest rates, government debt-service requirements for new and refinanced debt would also decline. Moreover, with a lower interest rate structure, the value of the dollar might be depressed enough to elevate exports and reduce imports. This improvement in the balance of trade might in turn push upward on GNP and hence tax collections. Of course, these are only possible, and indeed, optimistic forecasts. Nevertheless, it is entirely conceivable that the above sequence of events, or some reasonable facsimile thereof, would not only directly act to reduce the deficit, but might also permit sufficient growth in the economy to offset the potentially depressing effects on the economy as a whole of genuine deficit reduction policies by the Congress and the President.

Of course, such a scenario is possible, but not necessarily very probable. For instance, how expansionary should the monetary policy be? If excessively expansionary, inflation problems and inflationary expectations could severely or totally undermine policy effectiveness. Moreover, if an expansionary monetary policy acts to reduce interest rates, just how low can they fall and how rapidly can they fall? There are limits! And, if would-be borrowers come to perceive a policy of more or less continuous interest rate drops, they may come to expect future interest rate drops and thus may attempt to postpone borrowing and the spending it might finance. Similar expectations on the part of lenders may further complicate the picture. Recessionary potential, with all that it entails, might ensue. Or, at the least, a slowdown might occur.

Overview

Chapter 6 described, in theoretical terms, the concept of crowding out, which could be characterized as complete, partial, or zero. Chapter 7 empirically examined whether there was evidence to substantiate the existence of a crowding out effect from deficits. In chapter 7, it was clearly established that crowding out does occur. Indeed, although the techniques adopted are entirely different, chapter 7 generated conclusions that are entirely consistent with those in Cagan (1985) and Feldstein and Eckstein (1970). It has also been argued that although crowding out does apparently occur, it is only partial (see Cagan, 1985; Abrams and Schmitz, 1978; Arestis, 1979; Cebula, 1985; and Zahn, 1978). That is, although it appears that deficits may carry with them some adverse side effects, there are nonetheless typically positive net benefits to the economy as a whole in terms of economic growth and expansion. Stated differently, were the increases bad in public spending and private spending associated with the enormous deficits of calendar year 1982 on balance? Hardly. The deficit of 1982 must in any reasonable evaluation be given much of the credit for pulling our economy out of the 1981/1982 recession. It is our view, then, that crowding out does occur; that it must logically only be partial; and that on balance most deficits tend to directly or indirectly stimulate the economy.

This chapter has warned of the potential dangers of combating the deficit through tax increases or diminished government spending. In terms of the 1981/1982 recession, for example, efforts to balance the federal budget in 1982 would have had very destructive consequences. Had the deficit been eradicated by either higher taxes or diminished government outlays, the outcome would have been reduced private and/or public spending with no exodus from the recession, and quite likely a deepened (as well as prolonged) recession.

A few additional comments about the deficit and the national debt might now be in order. The current national debt is in the range of $2 trillion. Most of this debt is owned by American businesses and citizens, be it directly or through their financial institutions. If the federal government is poorer because it owes more, then the private sector of our economy is also better off (richer) in terms of its holdings of Treasury debt.[4] Presumably, people who view themselves as richer have a greater propensity to spend. If this line of reasoning is valid, then a huge national debt can, through a wealth effect, stimulate the economy. This in turn implies, once again, that although crowding out may occur (see chapter 7), there presumably are net positive benefits from federal debt and deficits.

Next, consider the role of inflation when evaluating the national debt and changes therein (deficits). Inflation alters the value of the national debt so that the size of the deficit per se exaggerates the growth of the real national debt. If the inflation occurs at a 5 percent annual rate, the real value of an existing $2 trillion debt is reduced by 5 percent, or $100 billion. With a deficit of, say, 180 billion current dollars, the total real debt rises by $180 billion less $100 billion, or only $80 billion (technically even less, since we also should deflate the deficit). A problem with deficits and the national debt may well exist, but really how big is it?

On the other hand, consider the aforementioned wealth effect together with the effects of inflation within the context of the Gramm-Rudman-Hollings Act. In accord with this legislation, let us assume that the deficit is eliminated as of 1991. With zero inflation, the real value of the national debt would be unchanged in 1991. However, if there is any inflation whatsoever during 1991, the real value of the national debt would decline. This reduction in real wealth would reduce private sector purchasing power and thus private sector expenditures, and, as a result, contribute further to the adverse impacts that higher taxes or slowed federal government spending might have generated. Indeed, even if the deficit is not eliminated but is drastically reduced, only a modicum of inflation could yield these kinds of adverse wealth effects.

Earlier in this book, we have argued that deficits are not all good—there are adverse side effects associated with a deficit. However, it should also be clear that we must reject the notion that all deficits are bad. We need not be preoccupied with deficits and the national debt, nor, of course, should we be entirely complacent. As Cagan (1985, p. 218) warns, the financing and economic impacts of deficits appear to be somewhat unstable, and it is unclear as to how long credit markets will be able to continue absorbing large volumes of Treasury borrowings in the future without greater adverse side effects. And, Cagan further warns, while crowding out has to date been only moderate, this could change.

Notes

1. We conceivably could observe changes similar to those expected from the taxpayer revolt and Proposition 13 and Proposition 4.

2. Sales taxes are likely to lose their deductibility.

3. The list is altogether too lengthy to provide here. Nevertheless, the reader may find the budgetary proposals by the Heritage Foundation, edited by John Palffy (1985), of interest. Similarly, the Congressional Budget Office study (1985) is enlightening, as is the study by the *President's Private Sector Study on Cost Control* (Grace Commission, 1984).

4. Holding the stock of federal government assets fixed, an increase in the debt/asset ratio will raise the value of the claims of bond holders, ceteris paribus. Impounded in ceteris paribus, of course, is the aggregate price level.

References

Abrams, B.A., and M.D. Schmitz, 1978. The "Crowding Out" Effect of Government Transfers on Private Charitable Contributions, *Public Choice*, vol. 33, pp. 29–39.

Arestis, P., 1979. The "Crowding Out" of Private Expenditure by Fiscal Actions: An Empirical Investigation, *Public Finance/Finances Publiques*, vol. 34, pp. 19–41.

Cagan, P., 1985. *The Economy in Deficit*. Washington, D.C.: American Enterprise Institute.

Cebula, R.J., 1974. Local Government Policies and Migration: An Analysis for SMSAs in the United States, Public Choice, vol. 19, pp. 86–93.

Cebula, R.J., 1985. Crowding Out and Fiscal Policy in the United States: A Note on the Recent Experience, *Public Finance/Finances Publiques*, vol. 40, pp. 133–136.

Congress of the United States, Congressional Budget Office, 1985. *Reducing the*

Deficit: Spending and Revenue Options. Washington, D.C.: U.S. Government Printing Office.

Evans, P., 1985. Do Large Deficits Produce High Interest Rates? *American Economic Review,* vol. 75, pp. 68–87.

Feldstein, M., and O. Eckstein, 1970. The Fundamental Determinants of the Interest Rate, Review of Economics and Statistics, vol. 52, pp. 363–375.

Grace Commission, 1984. *President's Private Sector Survey on Cost Control.* Washington, D.C.: U.S. Government Printing Office.

Hoelscher, G., 1983. Federal Borrowing and Short Term Interest Rates, *Southern Economic Journal,* vol. 50, pp. 319–333.

King, A., 1978. The American Policy in the Late 1970s: Building Coalitions in the Sand, in *The New American Political System,* A. King (ed.). Washington, D.C.: American Enterprise Institute, pp. 371–396.

Makin, J.H., 1983. Real Interest, Money Surprises, Anticipated Inflation and Fiscal Deficits, *Review of Economics and Statistics,* vol. 65, pp. 374–384.

Mascaro, A., and A.H. Meltzer, 1983. Long- and Short Term Interest Rates in a Risky World, *Journal of Monetary Economics,* vol. 10, pp. 485–518.

Motley, B., 1983. Real Interest Rates, Money, and Government Deficits, *Federal Reserve Bank of San Francisco, Economic Review,* Summer, pp. 31–45.

Ostrosky, A., 1978. Some Economic Effects and Causes of State and Local Government Commitment to Public Education, *Review of Business and Economic Research,* vol. 14, pp. 68–72.

Pack, J.R., 1973. Determinants of Migration to Central Cities, *Journal of Regional Science,* vol. 13, pp. 249–260.

Palffy, J., 1985. *How to Slash $119 Billion from the Deficit.* Washington, D.C.: The Heritage Foundation.

Reese, T.J. 1980. *The Politics of Taxation.* Westport, Conn.: Quorum Books.

Surrey, S., 1957. The Congress and the Tax Lobbyist—How Special Tax Provisions Get Enacted, *Harvard Law Review,* vol. 70, pp. 1145–1182.

Zahn, F., 1978. A Flow of Funds Analysis of Crowding Out, *Southern Economic Journal,* vol. 45, pp. 195–206.

Index

About the Author

Richard J. Cebula is professor of economics at Emory University. He received the A.B. degree from Fordham College and the Ph.D. degree from Georgia State University. Dr. Cebula has published numerous articles in major scholarly journals in the fields of migration, regional economics, and macroeconomics. He is the author of *The Determinants of Human Migration* (Lexington Books, 1979) and *Geographic Living-Cost Differentials* (Lexington Books, 1983).